RURAL REVIVAL

Growing Churches in Shrinking Communities

W. Scott Moore

Rogersville, Alabama

First Edition

Rural Revival

Author: W. Scott Moore, B.B.A, M. Div., D. Min.
© 2012 by Eleos Press www.eleospress.com

Cover Art: W. Scott Moore
Cover Design: W. Scott Moore
Interior Formatting: Eleos Press www.eleospress.com

Also available in eBook form

Eleos Press publishes this volume as a document of critical, theological, historical, and/or literary significance and does not necessarily endorse or promote all the views or statements made herein, or verify the accuracy of any statements made by the Author. References to persons or incidents herein may have been changed to protect the identity of those involved.

ISBN-13: 978-0615650395

PRINTED IN THE UNITED STATES OF AMERICA

Note to the Reader

The research for this book was completed in 2003. The contents of this book are a snapshot of the various churches and church leaders at that point in time. Research materials cited are those that were then currently available. The churches studied were all Southern Baptist churches.

Nevertheless:

- The four primary growth factors outlined herein may be considered as timeless.
- The program recommendations will continue to be effective in the growth of rural churches.
- The ideas are transferrable to churches of all denominations that may truly be characterized as "Christian": those that follow the Lord Jesus Christ and seek to win others to faith in Him.

May God bless you, dear readers, as you work to grow His church.

Contents

INTRODUCTION

Most of the sixteen million Southern
Baptists were classified in a recent news article
as living in either suburban, small town, or rural
areas.[1] Phillip B. Jones, director of the Strategic
Planning Support Team of the North American
Mission Board, stated: "Most Southern Baptist
congregations are small and are located in small
towns and rural areas. Over a third are located
in rural or open country." He also observed,
"Slightly less than a third are located in small
towns and villages of less than 10,000
population."[2]

A few of these Southern Baptist churches
classified as "rural" have experienced a
significant numerical increase in average Sunday
school attendance. The primary purposes of this

---

[1]Julia Leiblich, "Southern Baptist President Urges Outreach"
<u>Athens Daily News</u> (Athens, GA: Online Athens) 16 June 1999.

[2]Philip B. Jones, <u>Southern Baptist Congregations Today</u> (Atlanta:
North American Mission Board, 2001), iii-iv.

---

project, therefore, are both to isolate and to apply the key growth principles that have been effectively used in these churches. Many secondary objectives were also established to fulfill this purpose.

The project consisted of several steps. First, the theological rationale for church growth was investigated.

Second, the term "rural" required a clear definition. This definition included the relationship between a rural community and its churches. This relationship was particularly scrutinized as to the limitations rural communities placed upon the growth of its resident local churches.

Third, a study was conducted to isolate growing rural churches from those with either a flat or declining membership. Leaders of the growing churches were polled for their impressions of reasons for the growth of their churches.

Fourth, the results of the polls from the church leaders were examined as to the significance of their responses. Only four responses were considered significant in the growth of the churches.

Fifth, the target church was studied. This step included the examination of the history and location of the church.

Sixth, the principles were applied to the church by two separate means. A team was selected to assist in visiting the seven growing churches and in the implementation of the four growth principles. The church was also involved through Sunday evening messages and an open forum meeting.

The Theological Rationale for Church Growth

Church growth is a scriptural principle. Jesus made three statements that subsequently validated the Church Growth Movement. The first statement, found in Matthew 28:18-20, is commonly identified as "the Great Commission." Jesus declared:

All power is given unto me in heaven and in earth. Go ye therefore, and teach all nations, baptizing them in the name of the Father, and of the Son, and of the Holy Ghost: Teaching them to observe all things whatsoever I have commanded you: and, lo, I am with you alway, even unto the end of the world. Amen.

C. Peter Wagner identified Donald A. McGavran as "the father of the Church Growth Movement."[3] McGavran and Winfield C. Arn concurred with Wagner's preceding conclusions: "Church growth begins in God's unswerving purpose to save men. . . . This purpose of God, shared by his servants, is the driving force behind Church Growth."[4]

Jesus' second statement regarding missions is found in John 17:18, "As thou hast sent me into the world, even so have I also sent

---

[3]Donald A. McGavran, Understanding Church Growth, 3d ed. Rev. and ed. C. Peter Wagner (Grand Rapids: Eerdmans, 1990), viii.

[4]Donald A McGavran and Winfield C. Arn, Ten Steps for Church Growth (San Francisco, CA: Harper and Row, 1977), 35.

them into the world." McGavran and Arn explained:

> *The purpose of the sending is clear. Five times in this prayer, the Lord expressed the idea that the basic purpose of His appointing and teaching and sending the disciples was that "the world may believe."* [5]

A third church growth passage, Acts 1:8, "continued to stress the evangelization of the world." [6] Jesus said in this verse:

> *But ye shall receive power, after that the Holy Ghost is come upon you: and ye shall be witnesses unto me both in Jerusalem, and in all Judaea, and in Samaria, and unto the uttermost part of the earth.*

McGavran stated, "The chief and irreplaceable purpose of mission is church

---

[5]McGavran and Arn, <u>Ten Steps for Church Growth.</u>, 36.

[6]Ibid.

growth."[7]   He succinctly concluded, "Among other characteristics of mission . . . the chief and irreplaceable one must be this: that mission is a divine finding, vast and continuous."[8]

Definition of "Rural"

What is a rural community? What are the characteristics of these communities? What are the environmental advantages and limitations to churches established in these communities?

Webster defined *rural* as, "of or relating to the country, country people or life, or agriculture."[9] The U.S. Census Bureau defined *rural* in terms of population density as, "places less than 2500."[10]   Rockwell C. Smith, former

---

[7]McGavran, Understanding Church Growth, 21-22.

[8]Ibid.

[9]Merriam Webster's Collegiate Dictionary, 10th Edition (Springfield, MA: Merriam-Webster, Inc., 1995), 1026.

[10]U.S. Department of Commerce, Bureau of the Census, Urban and Rural Definitions (Washington, D.C.: U.S. Census Bureau Online, 1995).

professor of sociology of religion at Garrett Theological Seminary in Evanston, Illinois described a rural community simply as, "the primary living space of its members."[11]

Characteristics of the Rural Community

A major distinguishing characteristic of a rural community is its power structure. William J. Gore and Leroy C. Hodapp asserted four types of rural power structures: one family and/or industry, cliques or coalitions, leadership pool, and absentee-owned corporations. The one family and/or industry leadership type "is exemplified by a dominant family or industry, which controls the major source of employment and the resources."[12]

---

[11]Rockwell C. Smith, <u>Rural Ministry and the Changing Community</u> (Nashville: Abindgon, 1971), 54.

[12]William J. Gore and Leroy C. Hodapp, eds., <u>Change in the Small Community: An Interdisciplinary Survey</u> (New York: Friendship Press, Inc., 1967), 50-52.

Cliques or coalitions are "made up of a relatively small number of community influentials." These *influentials* "emerge into . . . [a] clique group, which constitutes the primary policy-making structure of the community."[13]

The third power structure is a leadership pool. Gore and Hodapp alleged:

> *This system is a pluralistic type of community power structure. It includes a sizable number of able people who address themselves to a particular issue; however, few of these individuals are involved in a large number of issues.*[14]

Absentee-owned corporations are the fourth type of power structure. Leaders of these businesses were once a major influence in a rural community, but are now involved in those "rare issues where the parent corporation has some

[13]Gore and Hodapp, eds., Change in the Small Community: An Interdisciplinary Survey., 52.

[14]Ibid.

economic stake or where public relations programs are important."[15]

Advantages of the Rural Community

The rural congregation has three distinct environmental advantages. The first advantage is the perseverance of the rural church. Pegge Boehm and associates from the Center for Theology and Land: Rural Ministry Program at the Wartburg Theological Seminary in Dubuque, Iowa, concurred, "In numerous rural communities, the church is the most resilient institution." These authorities further maintained, "[The church] . . . is the 'convenor of community,' and out-survives even the local tavern!"[16]

---

[15]Gore and Hodapp, Change in the Small Community, 55.

[16]Pegge Boehm, et. al., Rural Ministry: The Shape of the Renewal to Come (Nashville: Abingdon, 1998), 21.

The second advantage of the rural church is a shared optimism among the congregants. Boehm and associates stated:

> *The church witnesses to a hope beyond decline; it remains realistically optimistic even in a depressing situation. It offers a vision that buoys the spirits of many rural peoples.*[17]

The third environmental advantage is the considerable absence of competition. Rural community residents must find "within its boundaries . . . the basic services which are needed to meet their individual and collective needs."[18]

This lack of competition has been threatened, however, in recent years. John D. Freeman with the Home Mission Board of the Southern Baptist Convention, maintained:

---

[17]Boehm, <u>Rural Ministry</u>., 21

[18]Ibid., 54.

Changes produced by new methods of travel and the industrial development have brought this about and, unless it is counteracted in some way, there will soon be little of genuine community spirit and interest left in multitudes of rural sections.[19]

Freeman further asserted, "In all too many country areas there are few common interests, no common meeting place and little sense of community responsibility."[20] This simply "means that the rural church needs to be more intentional about its role in building community than it once was."[21]

---

[19]John D. Freeman, Country Church: Its Problems and Their Solution (Atlanta: Home Mission Board, 1943), 103.

[20]Freeman, Country Church: Its Problems and Their Solution, 103.

[21]Boehm, Rural Ministry, 130.

Limitations of the Rural Community

Associated Press writer Doug Johnson, recounting the details of a recent report, stated, "The 1990s brought a tale of two Souths--one metropolitan and prosperous, the other rural and in serious trouble."[22] He continued, "Coastal towns have emerged as vacation havens while older textile towns are searching for a place in the new economy."[23]

The primary restriction imposed by the rural community upon the local church was a shrinking population base. David L. Dodson, Ferrel Guillory, Sarah Rubin, and Leah D. Totten are members of the Research Committee of Manpower Development Corporation, Inc.(MDC). MDC is a Chapel-Hill, North Carolina based think-tank that has studied

---

[22]Doug Johnson, "Sun Belt Prosperous, Poor," The Decatur Daily, 1 September 2002, sec. A, 1.

[23]Ibid., 1.

changes in the South since 1967. Dodson and associates asserted, "Since the end of World War II, the South has inexorably shifted from a largely rural to a predominately metropolitan region." Dodson corroborated this assertion with the fact that "nearly three-fourths of Southerners now live in metro areas."[24]

This population shift became more pronounced during the decade of the 1990s. MDC reported, "High-poverty rural counties lost thousands of young people and working-age adults to the South's growing cities." The remaining population at the time of the report consisted of those described as "place-bound people lacking education and skills sought by employers--high school dropouts, single mothers, and older adults."[25]

This document attributed the population shift to the loss of many former job opportunities in many rural districts. According to Johnson,

---

[24]William F. Winter, The State of the South 2002: Shadows in the Sunbelt Revisited, by (Chapel-Hill, NC: MDC Inc., 2002), 6, 16.

[25]Ibid., 8.

"The recession that ushered in the 21st century . . . hastened the collapse of traditional Southern industries."[26]

Dodson and associates asserted, "A simultaneous decline in agriculture and manufacturing had undermined the rural South's economic foundation."[27] According to Dodson, "between 1986 and 2000, textile employment in Southern states fell from 549,000 to 418,000. Apparel jobs plummeted even faster, from 536,000 to 259,000."[28] These figures accounted for the loss of more than 400,000 positions of employment!

An additional statistic illustrated the economic difficulties associated with the South. The investigators lamented that "the South is home to 44 percent of the nation's non-metro population but 51 percent of the nation's non-metro poor."[29]

---

[26]Johnson, "Sun Belt Prosperous, Poor," 1.

[27]Winter, The State of the South 2002, 3.

[28]Ibid., 10.

[29]Ibid., 8.

The farming economy has also suffered considerably in Southern states. Dodson announced, "Agricultural jobs fell from 17 percent of non-metro employment in the South in 1969 to 8 percent at the end of the 1990s."[30]

Economic problems have multiplied in rural communities due to the current state of technology. The result of this insufficient technological base has been a reduction in the economic competitiveness of rural areas.

Dodson and associates at MDC correspondingly commented, "The recent recession has not slowed the race toward a more knowledge-oriented economy."[31] They maintained:

> *Technology continues to transform all manner of industries--and the way places are organized--not only the so-called high-tech firms but also textiles and farming. Yet, most*

[30]Winter, The State of the South 2002., 11.

[31]Ibid., 5.

Southern states rank low on preparedness for the knowledge economy.[32]

A second limitation imposed upon a local church by a rural community is the stability of the rural neighborhood. These communities typically experience a minimal shift in population. This unchanging nature of neighborhoods can be a significant discouragement to church growth. Ezra Earl Jones declared:

> *Most of the residents in the community should have lived in their present homes for less than three years. Most people living in an area for longer than that have established themselves in another congregation or have become confirmed nonchurchgoers. Once the people have related themselves to another congregation, formed friendships, and taken*

---

[32]Winter, The State of the South 2002,, 26.

on responsibilities, it is difficult to attract them to the new congregation.[33]

A third limitation imposed by the rural community upon the local church was also related to the shrinking population base--the loss of leadership. According to Jones:

> *Historically [the owners of family farms and farm-related businesses] . . . were the source of much of the leadership in rural counties, from elected officials to volunteer firemen to PTA members. So the contraction of the agricultural sector has had civic as well as economic consequences.*[34]

---

[33]Ezra Earl Jones, Strategies for New Churches (New York: Harper & Row, 1976), 92.

[34]Ibid., 11.

THE STUDY

This project focuses upon rural churches in North Alabama that have experienced significant growth in average Sunday school attendance. Sunday school participation is a good indicator of comprehensive church health because:

> *Sunday school is the foundational strategy in a local church for leading people to faith in the Lord Jesus Christ and for building on-mission Christians through open Bible study groups that engage people in evangelism, discipleship, ministry, fellowship, and worship.*[35]

The decadal growth rate (DGR) used to select the churches was a minimum increase of 50 percent in average Sunday school attendance.

---

[35]Ken Hemphill and Bill Taylor, <u>Ten Best Practices To Make Your Sunday School Work</u> (Nashville: Lifeway Press, 2001), 13.

DGRs for average Sunday school attendance are determined as follows: subtract the 1991 figure from the 2001 figure; take the result and divide it by the 1991 figure; multiply that result by 100; the result is shown as a percentage.[36]

Two of the churches, however, have experienced a remarkable growth rate in a shorter period--Calvary Baptist Church and Sandy Creek Baptist Church. The DGR for these churches was computed by: clearing the calculator; dividing the 2001 Sunday school figure by the 1991 figure; pressing the y^x key on the calculator; pressing the $1/x$ key on the calculator, and then the = sign; pressing the y^x key again; pressing in the number of years under study (Calvary was for two years); multiplying the resulting figure by 100; subtracting 100 from that number; the result is shown as a percentage.[37]

---

[36]C. Peter Wagner and Bob Waymire, The Church Growth Survey Handbook, third edition (Colorado Springs, CO: Global Church Growth, 1984), 16.

[37]Wagner and Waymire, The Church Growth Survey Handbook, 17.

Case Studies of Growth

Five counties in north Alabama are classified as "rural." These counties have the lowest population density in north Alabama, with thirty-nine to sixty-one persons per square mile. The Cherokee, Franklin, Marion, Muscle Shoals, and Winston associations are found within these five counties. The Cherokee Baptist Association was organized in 1898. It was composed of forty churches at the end of the church year 2001.[38]

The Franklin Baptist Association was established in 1898. This association had thirty-five churches.[39]

The Muscle Shoals Baptist Association, established in 1820 was the oldest of the five associations. This association had thirty

---

[38]*2001 Annual Of the Alabama Baptist State Convention* (Montgomery, AL: Alabama Baptist State Board of Missions, 2002), 457.

[39]Ibid., 494.

churches.[40]   The target church, First Baptist Church of Town Creek, Alabama, is currently a member of this association.

The Winston Baptist Association was the largest of the five associations with forty-one churches.   Winston Association was established in 1874.[41]

The directors of Missions representing each of the five counties were contacted.   They all responded by providing the following statistics for member churches they believed were growing: average Sunday school attendance for church years 1991 and 2001.

The Response

Attendance in most of the rural churches from the five associations either leveled off or was in a state of decline.   Less than 9 percent of

[40]2001 Annual Of the Alabama Baptist State Convention, 517.
[41]Ibid., 554.

the congregations from the five rural associations in Alabama (twelve churches out of a combined total of one-hundred seventy-one) experienced a 50 percent growth rate in average Sunday school attendance during the church years 1991-2001 (see Table 1).

The twelve pastors were contacted; ten agreed to participate in the project. Four copies of a survey (Appendix A) were sent to the ten pastors along with a letter of additional explanation and a self-addressed, stamped envelope.

Table 1.
Growth Rate of Twelve Rural Churches

Association	Church	Start/End	Growth Rate
Cherokee	East Centre	65/110	69%/10 years

Cherokee	Gaylesville	4/15	275%/10 years
Cherokee	Sandy Creek	31/40	125%/5 years
Franklin	Calvary	152/214	453%/2 years
Franklin	Jonesboro	37/90	143%/10 years
Franklin	North Russellville	45/66	147%/10 years
Marion	South Hamilton	33/72	118%/10 years
Muscle Shoals	Hillsboro	35/114	226%/10 years
Muscle Shoals	New Zion	35/70	100%/10 years

Winston	FBC Double Springs	109/165	51%/10 years
Winston	Mt. Ebron	30/92	207%/10 years
Winston	New Prospect	91/142	156%/10 years

Eight of the ten churches responded, and thus became part of the study. All eight churches were classified by the leadership as blue-collar congregations. They were also classified by the Annual Church Profile as "white, non-Hispanic" congregations.[42]

---

[42]LifeWay Christian Resources, Annual Church Profile (Nashville: Southern Baptist Directory Services Online, 2001).

Participating Churches

Four of five associations contacted were represented in the study. The eight participating churches included: East Centre, Calvary, Jonesboro, North Russellville, Hillsboro, New Zion, First Baptist Double Springs, and New Prospect.

All eight churches experienced not only significant numerical growth but also remarkable financial gains beyond the 1991-2001 inflation rate of 30 percent. This figure was derived from the Consumer Price Index Calculator. The U.S. Bureau of Labor Statistics stated:

> *This instrument uses the average Consumer Price Index for a given calendar year. This data represents changes in prices of all goods*

and services purchased for consumption by urban households.[43]

CHEROKEE ASSOCIATION

Three churches from the Cherokee Association were contacted for the survey. Leaders from the East Centre Baptist Church were the only participants.

East Centre Baptist Church

East Centre Baptist Church is located at 1220 East Main Street (also the mailing address) in Centre, Alabama. The church was organized in 1949. According to the U.S. Census Bureau, the latest population figure was 3,216.[44]

---

[43]U.S. Bureau of Labor Statistics, Inflation Calculator, (Washington, D.C.: U.S. Department of Labor Online, 2000).
[44]U.S. Department of Commerce, Census of Population 2000 (Washington, D.C.: U.S. Census Bureau Online, 2000).

The current pastor, John Allen, has served since 1998.[45] He was the only participant in the survey.

Sunday school average attendance grew from 65 in 1991 to an average of 110 in 2001. Total offerings also increased from $78,215.00 in 1991 to $208,908.00 in 2001, a gain of 167 percent.[46]

FRANKLIN ASSOCIATION

The churches surveyed within the Franklin Association included Calvary, Jonesboro, and North Russellville Baptist Churches. All three churches are within the city limits of Russellville. The population of Russellville, as of 2000, was 8,971.[47]

---

[45]Lifeway, <u>Annual Church Profile</u>.
[46]Ibid.
[47]U.S. Department of Commerce, <u>Census 2000</u>.

Calvary Baptist Church

Calvary Baptist Church was established in 1960. It is located at 12641 Highway 43.

The two participants in the survey included the pastor, Matt Hall, and a member named Andy Richardson. Sunday school average attendance grew from 152 in 1999 to an average of 214 in 2001. Total offerings also increased from $295,273.00 in 1999 to $438,518.00 in 2001, a gain of 49 percent.[48]

Jonesboro Baptist Church

Jonesboro Baptist Church was founded in 1920. The church is located at 5061 Waterloo Road.

The three participants in the survey included: the pastor, Tom Wimberly; the Sunday school director, Nolanda N. Lindsey; and the

---

[48]Lifeway, <u>Annual Church Profile</u>.

Discipleship Training director, Mark J. Daniel. Sunday school average attendance grew from thirty-seven in 1991 to an average of ninety in 2001. Total offerings also showed an increase from $28,965.00 in 1991 to $88,319.00 in 2001, a gain of 205 percent.[49]

North Russellville Baptist Church

North Russellville Baptist Church was founded in 1941. The church is located at 1401 Waterloo Road.

Four people participated in the survey, including: the pastor, DeWayne Crumley, two deacons: Robert L. Jones and Thomas Uptain, and the pastor's wife, Sherry Crumley (also a Sunday school teacher and in charge of the Ladies' Ministries in the church). Sunday school average attendance grew from nine in 1991 to an average of forty-five in 2001. Total offerings also

---

[49]Lifeway, Annual Church Profile.

increased from $29,335.00 in 1991 to $51,028.00 in 2001, a gain of 74 percent.[50]

MUSCLE SHOALS ASSOCIATION

Two churches were surveyed from the Muscle Shoals Baptist Association. They were Hillsboro Baptist Church and New Zion Baptist Church.

Hillsboro Baptist Church

Hillsboro Baptist Church was founded in 1873. The church is located at 297 Rainzi Street in Hillsboro, Alabama. Hillsboro is a town with a 2000 population of 608.[51]

---

[50]Lifeway, Annual Church Profile.
[51]U.S. Department of Commerce, Census 2000.

The church did not have a pastor at the time of the survey. Participants included Randy Burns (the youth pastor), Forrest Garrison (the chairman of deacons), and Ronald G. Finger, (the Sunday school director).

Sunday school average attendance at Hillsboro grew from thirty-five in 1991 to an average of 114 in 2001. Total offerings also increased from $42,635.00 in 1991 to 171,000.00 in 2001, a gain of 301 percent.[52]

New Zion Baptist Church

New Zion Baptist Church was founded in 1931. The church is at 454 County Road 129 in Hatton, Alabama (but is still a part of the Muscle Shoals Baptist Association). Hatton is a town with a 1990 population of 4,218.[53]

---

[52]Lifeway, Annual Church Profile.
[53]U. S. Department of Commerce. U.S. Gazetteer. Washington, DC: U.S. Census Bureau Online. 20 October 2000.

The three participants from New Zion Baptist Church in the survey consisted of Pastor Roger Houston, Malcolm F. Wallace (a deacon, Sunday school teacher, and the Treasurer), and Doris Craig (a deacon's wife, choir member, and Vacation Bible school teacher). Sunday school average attendance at New Zion grew from thirty-five in 1991 to an average of seventy in 2001. Total offerings also increased from $29,755.00 in 1991 to $74,300.00 in 2001, a gain of 150 percent.[54]

WINSTON ASSOCIATION

Two churches were surveyed from the Winston Association. They included First Baptist Church of Double Springs and New Prospect Baptist Church.

---

[54]Lifeway, <u>Annual Church Profile</u>.

First Baptist Church, Double Springs

First Baptist Church was founded in 1906. The church is at 197 Main Street in Double Springs, Alabama. Double Springs is a town with a 2000 population of 1,003.[55]

Four people took part in the survey. The group consisted of George Whitten, the pastor, Michael H. Curtis, a deacon, Rebecca Crumpton, a substitute Sunday school teacher, co-director of Women on Mission, and Prayer Committee Chairperson, and Sheila Wallace, a member.

Sunday school average attendance at First Baptist grew from 109 in 1991 to an average of 165 in 2001. Total offerings also increased from $141,735.00 in 1991 to $318,242.00 in 2001, a gain of 125 percent.[56]

---

[55]U.S. Department of Commerce, <u>U.S. Gazetteer</u>.
[56]Lifeway, <u>Annual Church Profile</u>.

New Prospect Baptist Church

New Prospect Baptist Church was founded in 1924. The church is at 202 County Road 3463 in Haleyville, Alabama. Haleyville, Alabama, is a town with a 2000 population of 4,182.[57]

Three members of New Prospect contributed to the results of the survey: Ron Horton (the pastor), Teresa Ward (a Youth Leader), and Chris Brannon (the Small Group Leader). Sunday school average attendance at New Prospect grew from ninety-one in 1991 to an average of 142 in 2001. Total offerings also increased from $48,315.00 in 1991 to $153,386.00 in 2001, a gain of 217 percent.[58]

---

[57]U.S. Department of Commerce, <u>Census 2000</u>.
[58]Lifeway, <u>Annual Church Profile</u>.

PRINCIPLES INVOLVED IN RURAL CHURCH GROWTH

The Survey

A survey was designed (see Appendix A), using growth criteria found primarily in a chart entitled "What Factors Led You to Choose This Church?" contained in a recent book by Thom Rainer.[59] Twelve criteria were selected. Each question was rated regarding the growth of the

---

[59]Thom S. Rainer, <u>Surprising Insights From the Unchurched and Proven Ways To Reach Them</u> (Grand Rapids: Zondervan, 2001), 21.

church: no significance, minor significance, moderate significance, or major significance. The twelve criteria consisted of: local population growth, evangelistic programs, lay leadership, children's or youth ministries, a sense of God's presence in the service, the pastor and preaching, location of the church, worship style and music, a strong sense of "community," the Sunday school organization, the doctrinal position of the church, and the friendliness of the church membership.

The Analysis

Twenty-three pastors and lay leaders responded from the eight churches. Their responses were listed by churches in Appendix B; the totals were then recorded in Table 2 below.

Table 2. Overall Totals

Question	None	Minor	Moderate	Major	Total
1	11	8	3	1	23
2	0	11	8	4	23
3	0	7	10	5	22
4	0	3	10	10	23
5	0	0	3	20	23
6	0	0	9	14	23
7	11	10	2	0	23
8	2	7	10	4	23
9	3	7	7	6	23
10	1	7	14	1	23
11	0	5	6	12	23
12	0	0	5	18	23

The most significant response to each of the twelve questions would obviously be the "major" category. Several questions were answered with this response.

Significance of the Responses

The next step was to decide the significance of the participants' responses. Two possible methods could have been chosen.

First, the responses could have been ranked in descending order, beginning with the question that received the highest number of responses in the "major" category. The difficulty with this method, however, was its inability to prove the reliability of the responses as to whether they were statistically significant, or simply indiscriminate answers.

A second method was selected, the "t-distribution." This statistical method was developed by William Sealy Gosset. He designed this statistical method because he, "was working with small samples."[60]

Gosset consequently stated:

> *But as we decrease the number of experiments, the value of the standard deviation found from the sample of experiments becomes itself subject to an increasing error, until judgments reached in this way may become altogether misleading.*[61]

Gosset additionally alleged that:

> *The fundamental concepts concerning the part to be played by the theory of probability in drawing inferences from statistical data needed to be defined on a more logical basis than when the samples were large.*[62]

---

[60]E. S. Pearson, "Student": A Statistical Biography of William Sealy Gosset, eds. R. L. Plackett and G. A. Barnard (Oxford, England: Clarendon Press, 1990), 15-17.
[61]Ibid., 45.
[62]Ibid., 72.

This instrument was chosen from among several other statistical methods due to the limited number of responses (twenty-three). M. Fogiel, director of the Research and Education Association, asserted:

> *For large samples with* n≥30, *the sampling distributions were approximately normal. For small samples with* n≤30, *this approximation is inaccurate and becomes worse as the number of measurements* n *increases.* [63]

Martin Sternstein, Professor of Mathematics at Ithaca College, located in Ithaca, New York, reasoned, "Confidence intervals estimating and hypothesis testing using small samples involve the Student t-distribution."[64] He additionally explained the effectiveness of

---

[63]M. Fogiel, <u>Super Review of Statistics</u> (Piscataway, NJ: Research and Education Association, 2002), 195.
[64]Martin Sternstein, <u>Statistics</u> (Hauppauge, NY: Barron's Educational Series, Inc., 1994), 104.

the instrument, "Because the sample size is below thirty, we must use the t-distribution."[65]

The t-distribution was determined by the process contained in Appendix C--Sample Computations. The final answer (for question one--11.51) was the number that must be exceeded to be statistically significant. Since the highest response to question one was eleven, and that reply was in the "none" category, item one was therefore considered insignificant.

The same equation was applied to all twelve questions. The responses were examined for randomness. The purpose was to ensure that the responses were not arbitrarily selected. Webster defined the word "arbitrary" as, "depending on individual discretion and not fixed by law; existing or coming about seemingly at random or by chance or as a capricious and unreasonable act of will."[66]

---

[65]Sternstein, <u>Statistics.</u>, 107.
[66]<u>Merriam Webster's Collegiate Dictionary, 10th Edition</u> (Springfield, MA: Merriam-Webster, Inc., 1995) 58.

The Four Critical Responses

Four responses were deemed to be significant in the "major" category with a 90 percent level of confidence (see Table 3). Any number falling below this confidence level was simply categorized as a random response. Martin Sternstein identified the term "confidence" in the following terms:

> *Using a measurement from a sample, we will never be able to say exactly what the population proportion is; we will always say we have a certain confidence that the population proportion lies in a certain interval.*[67]

Question number five had the highest number above the minimum response, "a sense of God's presence in the church." This number

---

[67]Sternstein, <u>Statistics</u>, 123.

was a quantity of 2.96 higher than the minimum of seventeen needed.

Table 3. Significance of Responses

Response Number	Response Area	90% Confidence	High Response/ Significant--Rating
1	Population Growth	11.51	11/No
2	Evangelism	11.37	11/No
3	Lay Leadership	10.74	10/No
4	Children/Youth	11.70	10/No
5	God's Presence	17.04	20/Yes--1
6	Pastor/Preaching	13.91	14/Yes--4
7	Location of Church	12.29	11/No

8	Worship/Music	9.87	10/No*
9	Sense of Community	7.99	7/No
10	Sunday school	12.43	14/No*
11	Doctrinal Position	11.54	12/Yes--3
12	Friendliness	15.75	18/Yes--2

*Response numbers 8 and 10 are not considered significant because the high responses were ranked "3", only contributing moderately to the growth of the churches.

The number two response was to question number twelve: "friendliness of the church membership." This result exceeded the minimum response by a quantity of 2.75.

The third response was, "the doctrinal position of the church." The result was a quantity of .46 higher than the minimum required to be considered worthwhile.

A fourth, and final, response was to question number six, "the pastor and preaching." This response was a marginal quantity of .09 above the minimum to be considered statistically significant.

GROWTH FACTOR ONE-- GOD'S PRESENCE

A sense of God's presence in the church was the number one reason given by respondents for the growth of their respective rural churches. Roger Houston ranked this factor as the most important to the growth of the New Zion Baptist Church. He remarked:

> *The evident love for God and love for each other has contributed to our growth. There is a peace and warmth because of the Holy Spirit's presence. The people work together,*

support each other, and support me--which has drawn new people to [our church].[68]

Doris Craig also ascribed much of the church's growth to this factor. She observed, "I can feel God's presence in our church, and I know this has an impact on the growth of any church."[69]

Two experts disagreed with the primacy of God's presence. Wagner stated, "The primary catalytic factor for growth in the local church is the pastor."[70] Rainer concurred, "The formerly unchurched told us nine times out of ten times that the pastor was key in their entering the ranks of the churched."[71]

Barna's research contradicted both Wagner's and Rainer's findings. He revealed the unwillingness of pastors to accept the credit for

---

[68]W. Scott Moore, "Growth Survey" (Town Creek, AL: First Baptist Church, 2002), 1, photocopied.
[69]Ibid.
[70]C. Peter Wagner, <u>Your Church Can Grow: Seven Vital Signs of a Healthy Church</u>, second edition (Ventura, CA: Regal, 1984), 61.
[71]Rainer, <u>Surprising Insights From the Unchurched</u>, 56.

the growth of their churches, "Any success we experience in reaching the unchurched has more to do with allowing the Holy Spirit to work than it relies upon our own skills and cleverness."[72] Barna contended:

> *According to the leaders of the churches that are doing effective work among the unchurched, the environment of the church and the attitude and spiritual commitment of the congregants are more important than the pastor and the preaching.*[73]

Participants in the survey for this project did not dispute the importance of the pastor and preaching in church growth. The respondents rated the component as less significant than the growth factor of the presence of God.

The reason for this discrepancy is the extreme resistance to change found in many

---

[72]George Barna, Re-Churching the Unchurched (Ventura, CA: Issachar Resources, 2000), 125.
[73]Ibid.

rural churches. Ron S. Lewis stated, "It would be easier to reach a group of practicing Muslims than to turn a rural First Baptist Church around."[74] Dan Reiland conversely maintained, "I strongly believe that God's heart is in the revival of many, perhaps thousands, of His churches across the country."[75]

One reason for this resistance to change is the longevity of the typical rural church. Gary Farley asserted, "The life expectancy of a metropolitan church is about fifty years. Contrast that with a rural church whose life expectancy may be centuries."[76]

Farley continued, "Most older churches have developed bell cows--matriarchs and patriarchs who have carried them through

---

[74]Ron S. Lewis, interview by North American Church Growth Class, Germantown, TN, 23 September 1999, handwritten notes.

[75]Dan Reiland, "Mergers and Turnarounds (Part Two)" The Pastor's Coach: Equipping the Leaders of Today's Church, Vol. III, No. 18.

[76]"How The Family Church Grows: Honest Talk About Leading Change In The Smaller Congregation," Leadership Journal XIX (Spring 1998): 111.

difficult times."[77] He asserted, "[Many pastors] arrive with a kind of military mindset: 'I'm ordained, I'm going to lead, and this old guy needs to get out of my way.'"[78]

A second reason the presence of God is needed to produce changes for growth in these churches is many are dominated by the leadership of a few families. Leith Anderson stated that:

> *Their billboards may say "Welcome," but the visitor soon discovers that the only way to be fully assimilated and achieve influence is by marrying someone already in the church. Everybody is related.*[79]

A third obstacle to implementing the changes needed for rural church growth is the

---

[77]How The Family Church Grows."
[78]Ibid.
[79]Leith Anderson, <u>Dying for Change: An Arresting Look at the New Realities Confronting Churches and Para-Church Ministries</u> (Minneapolis: Bethany House, 1990), 113.

unwillingness of current members to accept new members. Martin Giese stated:

> *An elderly lady said [to me], "I just don't know anyone around here anymore." What she meant was "I no longer can catch up with everyone's life on a Sunday morning."*

The presence of God is contingent upon several elements. These ingredients include corporate involvement in worship, prayer, singing, and preaching.

The Importance of Worship

The Bible clearly teaches that God is present where He is worshiped. David wrote in Psalm 22:3, "But thou art holy, O thou that inhabitest the praises of Israel."

Gary Burge defined worship as, "an encounter in which God's glory, Word, and grace are unveiled, and we respond, in songs and prayers of celebration."[80]   He stated that people are searching for "worship that becomes familiar but not trite, that employs dignified language but is not stilted, language that is planned but is not mechanical."[81]

The Importance of Prayer

Many church leaders have agreed that the primary requirement for God's presence in a service is prayer. McGavran contended, "While an evangelical awakening . . . depends on the initiative of almighty God, it is usually granted to those who pray earnestly for it."[82]   Gary McIntosh stated, "There is no biblical church growth apart from the work of the Holy

---

[80]Gary M. Burge, "Are Evangelicals Missing God at Church?" Christianity Today, 6 October 1997, 20.

[81]Ibid.

[82]Donald A. McGavran, Understanding Church Growth, 3d ed. Rev. and ed. C. Peter Wagner (Grand Rapids: Wm. B. Eerdmans, 1990), 134.

Spirit."[83] Jesus announced in Matthew 21:13, "It is written, My house shall be called the house of prayer." Ezra stated in 2 Chronicles 7:1:

> *Now when Solomon had made an end of praying, the fire came down from heaven, and consumed the burnt offering and the sacrifices; and the glory of the LORD filled the house.*

Members of the First Baptist Church of Double Springs recognized the need for prayer. Sheila Wallace asserted, "Mind you, it has not been an easy chore--but through much prayer and seeking God's face as a church we continue to grow."[84] Rebecca Crumpton further commented:

> *I believe prayer is the most important thing in any church--persistent prayer--heart-felt*

---

[83]Gary L. McIntosh, "Biblical Church Growth: Growing Faithful Churches In the Third Millenium," Journal Of Evangelism And Missions, 1 (Spring 2002): 68.
[84]Moore, "Growth Survey," 1.

prayer--for ourselves, our pastor, our nation. But to get answers we must believe God and obey Him.[85]

Rob Jackson, an evangelism associate in the Office of Evangelism for the Alabama Baptist Convention and the former associate pastor of Buck Run Baptist Church in Jonesboro, Kentucky stated:

God is doing some unbelievable things at Buck Run because His people are daring to open up the channel for the power of the Holy Spirit to flow. They are paying the price in prayer."[86]

John Maxwell concurred: "Whenever God's presence comes down within the church,

---

[85]Moore, "Growth Survey," 1.
[86]Thom S., Eating the Elephant: Bite-Sized Steps To Achieve Long-Term Growth In Your Church (Nashville: Broadman and Holman, 1994), 115.

it lifts up the people spiritually. And that's when great things begin to happen."[87]

Jesus validated both Jackson's and Maxwell's statements. Serving as the supreme authority in Matthew 18:19-20, Jesus says:

> *Again I say unto you, That if two of you shall agree on earth as touching any thing that they shall ask, it shall be done for them of my Father which is in heaven. For where two or three are gathered together in my name, there am I in the midst of them.*

Jim Cymbala may have discovered the close link between prayer and the presence of God in a church service. He observed: "God is attracted to weakness. He can't resist those who

---

[87]John Maxwell, <u>Partners In Prayer: Support and Strengthen Your Pastor and Church Leaders</u> (Nashville: Thomas Nelson, 1996), 96-97.

humbly and honestly admit how desperately they need him."[88]

Church members who follow Jan Karon's admonition regarding the frequency of prayer would regularly experience the presence of God in their worship services. She stated, "St. Paul exhorts us to 'pray without ceasing'--in short, while playing, running, working, cooking, resting, and even, surely, while watching television."[89]

Prayer is a term that is much used and often misunderstood. Many church members see it as an attempt to persuade God to act in accordance with the desires of the petitioner.

Some Christians believe prayer is something to be observed only occasionally. A popular definition limits prayer as simply "an

---

[88]Jim Cymbala, Fresh Wind, Fresh Fire: What Happens When God's Spirit Invades the Hearts of His People (Grand Rapids: Zondervan, 1997), 19.
[89]Jan Karon, "Praying In Prime Time" World Vision Today (Autumn 2002), 31.

address (as a petition) to God . . . in word or thought."[90]

The best understanding of the meaning of prayer can be found in the Bible. Definitions of the five Old Testament and the three New Testament words most commonly translated as "prayer" (in the King James Version of the Bible) are helpful.

The five Old Testament words for prayer are: האיש, השאהאל, לאלאפ, האללהפת, and ראהתא. האללהפ was the most widely used Old Testament word for prayer, employed in that capacity a total of seventy-seven times. האללהפ meant "[to] pray a prayer[,] a house of prayer, [or to] hear or listen to [a] prayer."[91]

The four words האיש, השאהאל, לאלאפ, and ראהתא were each translated "prayer" once. לאלאף, rendered prayer seventy-four times, meant "to intercede [or] to pray." השאהאל, means "[the] whisper[ing] (of [a] prayer)." האיש

---

[90]<u>Merriam-Webster's Collegiate Dictionary</u>, 914.
[91]R. Laird Harris, Gleason L. Archer, Jr., and Bruce K. Waltke, eds. <u>Theological Wordbook of the Old Testament</u>, vol. A (Chicago: Moody, 1980), 1776.

had the conception of "meditation, complaint, [or] musing[; to] talk." Harris and associates defined ראההתא as, "to pray, entreat, supplicate[;] to make supplication, [to] plead."[92]

The Old Testament idea of prayer, then, was much broader than the popular definition of a petition. It also included the place of prayer, the listening aspect of prayer, prayer for the needs of others, and meditation.

Three New Testament words and their derivatives, προσευχη, δεησισ, and εντευξισ, were also translated as "prayer" in the King James Version of the Bible. The most commonly used word (thirty-nine times), προσευχη, meant a "prayer addressed to God."[93]

The second most widely translated word as "prayer" was the word δεησισ. Δεησισ, used

---

[92]Harris, Theological Wordbook., 1107, 1722, 1776, 2255.
[93][Carl Ludwig] Grimm and [Christian Gottlob] Wilke, Greek-English Lexicon of the New Testament, trans. and rev. Joseph Henry Thayer (New York: American Book Co., 1889; reprint, Grand Rapids: Zondervan, 1981), 117, 545.

twelve times, meant "seeking, asking, entreating, entreaty."[94]

The third word, εντευξισ, was defined as "prayer" only twice in the New Testament. Εντευξισ carried the idea of "an interview, a coming together . . . , that for which an interview is held, a conference or conversation, a petition, supplication."[95] This word was helpful in recognizing the two-way aspect of communication with God.

Thayer compared the three synonyms in addition to their general definitions. He gave them the following shades of meaning: προσευχη "is unrestricted in its contents," is "limited to prayer to God," and includes "the element of devotion."[96]

Δεησισ, contrastingly, is primarily petitionary in nature. It may "be used of a request addressed to man," and "gives

---

[94]Grimm and Wilke, Greek-English Lexicon, 126.
[95]Ibid, 132.
[96]Ibid., 126.

prominence to the expression of personal need."[97]

Εντευςισ "expresses confiding access to God." It centers on the "childlike confidence" a believer should have when entering the presence of God.[98]

The New Testament usage, therefore, contributes two additional thoughts to both the Old Testament idea and the popular definition. One thought involves the idea of pleading with God. This extends the notion of prayer to more than just a dispassionate statement of one's need to God.

The other thought found exclusively in the New Testament is that of a "conference with God." The petitioner speaks with God, confident that He is listening to the requests.

---

[97]Grimm and Wilke, <u>Greek-English Lexicon</u>,.
[98]Ibid.

The Importance of Singing

Respondents from the seven growing rural churches indicated that worship style was insignificant in the growth they experienced. The genre of music may be unimportant, but singing remains crucial to a worship experience.

The hymn book of the Bible (the Psalms) contains several admonitions to sing praises to the Lord. David stated in Psalm 7:17, "I will praise the LORD according to his righteousness: and will sing praise to the name of the LORD most high." He continued in Psalm 9:2, "I will be glad and rejoice in thee: I will sing praise to thy name, O thou most High." David declared in Psalm 18:49, "Therefore will I give thanks unto thee, O LORD, among the heathen, and sing praises unto thy name." He acknowledged in Psalm 21:13, "Be thou exalted, LORD, in thine own strength: *so* will we sing and praise thy power." David stated in Psalm 27:6, "And now shall mine head be lifted up above mine enemies round about me: therefore will I offer in his tabernacle sacrifices of joy; I will sing, yea, I will sing praises unto the LORD." Other Psalms encouraging the singing of praises include: 30:12, 33:2, 47:6, 47:7, 57:7, 57:9, 61:8, 66:2, 68:4, 68:32, 71:22, 75:9, 92:1, 98:4, 104:33, 108:1, 108:3, 135:3, 138:1, 144:9, 146:2, 147:1, 147:7, 149:1, and 149:3.

The Importance of Preaching

Respondents from the seven growing rural churches indicated that preaching was particularly significant in the growth they experienced. This overlaps, to some degree, the fourth growth factor of the pastor and preaching.

Preaching, according to the Bible, is crucial to the establishment of faith. Paul announced in Romans 10:14, "How then shall they call on him in whom they have not believed? and how shall they believe in him of whom they have not heard? and how shall they hear without a preacher?" He further maintains in Romans 10:17, "So then faith *cometh* by hearing, and hearing by the word of God." He concluded with the corresponding declaration in 1 Corinthians 1:21, "For after that in the wisdom of God the world by wisdom knew not God, it pleased God by the foolishness of preaching to save them that believe."

GROWTH FACTOR TWO--
FRIENDLINESS

Friendliness of the membership was the second response. People are searching for friendly churches. Charles L. Yarborough, retired minister of First Christian Church in Albany, Kentucky, concurred with their assertion: "Before growth can occur you must have prospects, and you cannot get prospects if you don't have a friendly and receptive church."[99]   He stated most rural church members, "are friendly to their own members, but in truth, they often ignore the lonely visitor. They're so busy being neighborly to their neighbor, they pay no attention to others."[100] Boehm and associates agreed, "It sometimes comes close to being a place where 'everyone knows my name,' and cares about me and mine as I do about them and theirs."[101]

Charles Arn argued that people determine the friendliness of a church by, "how many people talk to them. The most important time for 'friendly talk' is immediately following the service."[102]

John C. Maxwell concurred with the need for friendliness in the church. He believed that,

---

[99]Charles Yarborough, "Hope In A No-growth Town: Realistic Help for Churches Facing Seemingly Impossible Odds," Leadership Journal, Summer 1996, 79.

[100]Yarborough, "Hope In A No-growth Town," 79.

[101]Pegge Boehm, Rural Ministry, 21.

[102]Charles Arn, "Second Impressions: Your Church Passed Their First Visit, But Will They Come Back?" Leadership Journal, Summer 2002, 11.

after the guest, the usher is the most important person in a church service:

> *The ushers are important because they are often the ones who have the first contact with people. They help people with directions. They are the ones who represent the church to newcomers.*[103]

Pastor Ron Horton attributed much of the growth of the New Prospect Baptist Church to the friendliness of the people. He confidently stated: "We have a good group of families with small children to youth. . . . Our people are very friendly and make visitors feel welcome."[104]

Nolanda N. Lindsey also gave high marks to friendliness on the survey. She commented that the church was, "a loving, caring, understanding worship center."[105]

---

[103]John C. Maxwell, <u>Ushers and Greeters</u> (El Cajon, CA: INJOY Ministries, 1991), 1-5.
[104]Moore, "Growth Survey," 1.
[105]Ibid.

Youth minister Randy Burns rated friendliness as the second most important growth factor at Hillsboro Baptist Church. He concluded: "Love among members is a very vital part of church growth. People need to be loved; if they find it at church, they will come back."[106] Michael H. Curtis, member of the First Baptist Church of Double Springs, concurred, "Our church has care and concern for our church family, as well as for those who have not yet come to know Jesus as their personal Savior."[107]

Doris Craig, a member of the New Zion Baptist Church, made a representative statement. She concluded, "The friendliness of the members is very important and has a major impact on the growth of our church."[108]

Ed Stetzer is the director of the Nehemiah Project Church Planting Center at the Southern Baptist Theological Seminary in Louisville, Kentucky. He referred to friendliness as a sense

---

[106]Moore, "Growth Survey," 1.
[107]Ibid.
[108]Ibid.

of "community." He stated *community,* "is a central value in most effective churches."[109] Stetzer continued:

> *This is good news for the church; community is central to its mission. With a culture eager for genuine community, the church of Christ can offer community with people and with God.*[110]

Thom Rainer and associates polled a category of persons whom they defined as "formerly unchurched." Eighty-eight percent of the 353 formerly unchurched respondents polled by this group said, "The friendliness of the people was a major attraction to the particular church they joined."[111]

Boehm and associates argued that the rural church "serves as a fellowship center and

---

[109]Bob Terry, "Ten Tips Identified For Postmodern Worship," The Alabama Baptist 12 April 2001.

[110]Terry, "Ten Tips Identified."

[111]Rainer, Surprising Insights, 96.

the base for many community initiatives."[112] They agreed with respondents that many rural churches excel in the attribute of friendliness.

GROWTH FACTOR THREE-- DOCTRINAL POSITION

The third ranked response was the doctrinal position of the church. Several growth experts recognized the importance of this factor. Schaller contended:

> *While some church shoppers, especially those who live alone and those who were born before 1935, place friendliness at the top of their list in evaluating churches, the vast majority place another criterion at the top: Does this congregation appear to be one that will be*

---

[112]Pegge Boehm, Rural Ministry, 21.

relevant and responsive to my religious needs?[113]

R. Albert Mohler, Jr. articulated the dilemma, "Americans have been negotiating away the core doctrines of the Christian faith--all the while claiming to remain Christians."[114] Many church members, therefore, no longer consider the clear teachings of the Bible as their standard for living. Barna confirmed this statement:

> *At least three out of ten born-again adults say that co-habitation, gay sex, sexual fantasies, breaking the speed limit or watching sexually explicit movies are morally acceptable.*[115]

---

[113]Lyle E. Schaller, "You Can't Believe Everything You Hear About Church Growth: Busting Common Myths About Expansion and Change," Christianity Today Winter 1997, 46.

[114]Tim Ellsworth, "Baptists Adrift in Doctrinal Confusion," SBC Life, October 2001, 5.

[115]George Barna, "Barna's Most Intriguing Findings," On Mission, May-June 2002, 43.

According to Rainer, however, "the formerly unchurched indicated a greater interest in doctrine than longer-term Christians."[116] Unchurched people, he continued, "were not just interested in the facts of the doctrine; they were insistent that the churches should be uncompromising in their stand."[117] The results of a poll corroborated these statements. Findings demonstrated, "Ninety-one percent of the formerly unchurched thought that doctrine was important."[118]

Barna explained the reason for the inquisitiveness of the unchurched population regarding the doctrinal perspective of the churches they visit. He announced, "Simply, they want to know if it is a Christian church, a cult or a non-Christian religion."[119]

---

[116]Rainer, <u>Surprising Insights</u>, 126,
[117]Ibid.
[118]Ibid., 127.
[119]George Barna, <u>Evangelism That Works: How to Reach Changing Generations with the Unchanging Gospel</u> (Ventura, CA: Regal, 1995), 65.

Barna further elucidated the need for doctrinal teaching, "Half of all adults argue that anyone who is 'generally good or does enough good things for others during their life will have a place in Heaven.'"[120]   He additionally observed, "[we have become] a nation whose theological views are increasingly inclusive of many faith traditions."[121]

Barna elaborated upon the facts of this doctrinal deficiency, "Six out of ten Americans reject the existence of Satan."[122]   He additionally commented, "A large minority of Americans believes that when Jesus Christ was on earth He committed sins."[123]   Barna concluded that, in this country, "A plurality of adults contends that, 'the Bible, the Koran, or the Book of

---

[120]George Barna, "Americans Draw Theological Beliefs from Diverse Points of View" <u>The Barna Update</u>, a bi-weekly email from George Barna (Ventura, CA: Barna Research), 8 October 2002.
[121]Ibid.
[122]Ibid.
[123]Ibid.

Mormon is all different expressions of the same spiritual truths."[124]

Lee Strobel was a self-proclaimed skeptic prior to his conversion to Christianity in 1981. He admitted that the reason for his personal investigation of the Christian religion was, "These people really believed this stuff. I didn't agree with them, but I couldn't dismiss their sincerity and conviction."[125]

GROWTH FACTOR FOUR-- PASTOR AND PREACHING

The fourth ranked response regarded the pastor and preaching. The pastor was perceived as influential in reaching people in the community. Barna defined the pastor as "one who understood the needs of the congregation

---

[124]Barna, "Americans Draw Theological Beliefs from Diverse Points of View."

[125]Lee Strobel, Inside the Mind of Unchurched Harry and Mary: How To Reach Friends and Family Who Avoid God and the Church (Grand Rapids: Zondervan, 1993), 200.

and the target audience and provided the necessary vision and spiritual guidance."[126]

Phillip B. Jones contended most Southern Baptist churches "have the services of an ongoing pastor--either regular or interim. Specifically, 83.3 percent of all congregations have a regular call[ed] pastor."[127] He additionally stated regarding the usual interim period, "Those congregations without a pastor have typically been without one for four months."[128]

Recent research suggested many pastors were well equipped for the task of leading the local church. Barna stated: "Since 1993, the number of pastors who say they have the spiritual gifts of preaching/teaching,

[126]George Barna <u>User Friendly Churches: What Christians Need To Know About the Churches People Love To Go To</u> (Ventura, CA: Regal, 1991), 143.

[127]Philip B. Jones, <u>Southern Baptist Congregations Today</u> (Atlanta: North American Mission Board, 2001), iv.

[128]Ibid.

pastor/shepherd, discernment and leadership has risen significantly."[129]

The importance of the pastor is proportionate to the size of the church. Church growth consultant Lyle Schaller contended, "The guiding generalization is that the larger the size of the congregation, the more important it is for the pastor to accept and fill the role of initiating leader."[130]

Pastor Ron Horton made reference to the significance of his own personal preaching style. He commented, "I normally preach expository messages through books of the Bible."[131]

John K. Allen of the East Centre Baptist Church claimed, "The right pastor with the right people participating in the right program has been the key."[132] He recognized pastoral leadership, therefore, as a significant catalyst for rural church growth.

---

[129]George Barna, "Barna's Most Intriguing Findings" On Mission May-June 2002, 42.
[130]Schaller, "You Can't Believe Everything," 46.
[131]Moore, "Growth Survey," 1.
[132]Ibid.

Randy Burns, the Youth Pastor at Hillsboro Baptist Church, agreed with Allen. He explained, "in order for the flock to grow they must be fed."[133] He additionally interjected: "Our people have been hungry for the Word and they have been fed well. A true church of Jesus Christ cannot grow without a healthy dose of the Word of God."[134] He concluded, "That (the preaching of the Bible) is the most important thing."[135]

New Zion Baptist Church member Doris Craig spoke about the importance of her pastor to the growth of the church. She contended, "We are blessed with a wonderful pastor and a great preacher as well, and I think the Pastor/Preaching [had] a major impact on the growth of our church."[136]

Two members of the First Baptist Church of Double Springs also believed in the importance of the pastor. The first member,

---

[133]Moore, "Growth Survey," 1.
[134]Ibid.
[135]Ibid.
[136]Ibid.

Michael H. Curtis, expressed his admiration for the pastor. He contended, "Our church has one of the most friendly and caring pastors I have ever known."[137] Curtis further added:

> *I have been involved in this church for approximately twenty-eight years. I have seen a lot of the ups and downs of church growth and decline, and feel one of the major factors in [the growth of] our church is the pastor.*[138]

The other respondent from First Baptist Church of Double Springs, Sheila Wallace, agreed with Curtis. She commented:

> *First Baptist Church has grown and continues to [grow] daily. I believe this is due to the leadership of our pastor. Bro. George came to our church with God's vision of what we needed to do for the Kingdom.*[139]

---

[137]Moore, "Growth Survey," 1.
[138]Ibid.
[139]Ibid.

THE TARGET CHURCH

First Baptist Church is located at 15770 Main Street (Alabama Highway 101) in Town Creek, Alabama. Town Creek, Alabama, had, as of 2000, a population of 1,216.[140] The church is situated less than one city block southeast of the primary business intersections of Alabama Highways 20 and 101.

The auditorium and parsonage cover most of the church property that faces the highway. The parking lot is located next to the church building both on the northwest corner and immediately behind the educational building and adjoining educational facilities. Additional parking is available on the street immediately west of the church property.

---

[140]U.S. Department of Commerce, 2000 Census of Population (Washington, D.C.: U.S. Census Bureau Online, 2000).

A Brief History of First Baptist Church

The 1971 Church Directory traced the roots of First Baptist Church to Liberty Church, a congregation that began around 1830. The church had no pastor from the end of the Civil War until it united with Pilgrim's Rest Church in September 1872. A remnant (forty-four members and two elders) constituted the new First Baptist Church in 1878.[141]

INITIAL LOCATION

The church was initially about ten miles northwest of Courtland, Alabama, near a place called "Red Bank." After the Civil War, the church was dismantled and rebuilt in the town formerly named "Jonesboro." The congregation

---

[141]1971 Directory of the First Baptist Church of Town Creek, Alabama (Waco, TX: United Church Directories, 1971).

was racially mixed; a description of the original building included "a balcony where Negroes were seated to worship."[142]

CURRENT LOCATION

Construction of the current structure at its present site began in July 1940. According to a statement in the 1971 Church Directory, "the church building now stands on a one acre plot donated by Fred Sykes."[143] Besides this original acre, "four lots have been purchased."[144] The church has received additional land donations and made an additional purchase; church grounds now cover approximately ten acres.

---

[142]1971 Directory of the First Baptist.
[143]Ibid.
[144]Book of Book of Memories(Town Creek, AL: The Welcome Home Committee, 1989), 160.

PASTORS

The average pastoral tenure has been less than four years. The church has had thirty-four pastors (including the current pastor) over its 124 year history.[145]

OBSTACLES TO GROWTH

Average Sunday school attendance at the First Baptist Church of Town Creek, Alabama, has shown a decline (-19% DGR) during the years 1991-2001. Six of the ten years under study show a decline in attendance. Offerings have fluctuated, with an overall increase over the ten-year period.

The greatest decline in Sunday school attendance, surprisingly, occurred in the 1999-

---

[145]1971 Directory.

2000 church year. This is disturbing considering the fact that, in the same year, resident membership has shown its greatest increase over the ten-year period. The Sunday school organization has clearly been unsuccessful in assimilating new church members over the last two years.

Age of the Church

First Baptist Church was formed in 1878. The church is, therefore, nearly 130 years old. Harry H. Fowler, a church growth consultant at the North American Mission Board of the Southern Baptist Convention, argued, "Old churches do not grow."[146]

Terry Stovall, using statistics derived from his study of 169 churches, contradicted

[146]Harry H.Fowler <u>Breaking Barriers of New Church Growth: Increasing Attendance from 0-150</u> (Rocky Mount, NC: Creative Growth Dynamics, Inc., 1988), 17.

Fowler's claim with the assertion, "The age of the church is not related to church growth. Older churches can be growing churches just as younger churches can decline."[147]

Many factors associated with the age of the church have contributed to the lack of growth. First, the church has tended to be very traditional. Some traditions have been helpful in the church's numerical growth and retention of members, including a strong sense of community, a family atmosphere, and a live Sunday morning radio broadcast.

Other traditions, however, have been restrictive to the addition of new members. One such tradition is the time of the worship service. First Baptist Church offers only one morning service at eleven o'clock. An additional eight o'clock service was introduced in the 1980s, but has since been eliminated.

---

[147]Terry Stovall, "A Study of the Differences Between Growing, Declining, Plateaued and Erratic Growth of Southern Baptist Churches in Texas," The Alabama Baptist, 7 February 2002, 3.

A second factor associated with the age of First Baptist church is the lower baptismal ratio associated with older churches. A Southern Baptist Convention report stated that, on the average, "churches over forty-one years old baptize [only] 3.5 persons per 100 members."[148] This tendency (see Table 4) has been shown throughout the 1991-2001 church years.

Table 4. Baptisms per 100 Members[149]

Church Year	Baptisms/ Total Membership	Baptisms per 100 members
1991	8/574	1.4
1992	7/563	1.2

[148]Fowler, Breaking Barriers, 23.
[149]LifeWay Christian Resources, Annual Church Profile

(Nashville: Southern Baptist Directory Services Online, 2001).

1993	9/564	1.6
1994	5/562	0.8
1995	10/566	1.8
1996	16/565	2.8
1997	14/575	2.4
1998	11/578	1.9
1999	18/577	3.1
2000	11/590	1.9
2001	20/590	3.3

A third factor associated with the age of the church that contributed to the lack of growth has been the aging of the membership. The young couples that formerly dominated the church twenty years ago are now aged early to mid-forties. Their teen-aged children have finished high school and many of these children have left the community.

These losses can be recovered. Stovall stated, "Neither the median age of the population nor the number of children in the neighborhood plays a significant role in whether a church is growing or declining."[150]

Staff Obstacles

First Baptist Church has employed historically only one full-time pastoral staff member. The church experienced significant growth during the years 1980-1990, but did not have the vision to add professional staff members. The ministerial staff of First Baptist Church includes a full-time pastor, a part-time minister of music, and a part-time minister of

---

[150]Terry Stovall, "A Study of the Differences," The Alabama Baptist, 7 February 2002, 3.

youth. Additional staff members include a part-time secretary, a part-time custodian, and two part-time maintenance workers.

Most of the growth problems have been attributed by church members to staff changes occurring during the early 1990s.[151] First, the pastoral changes throughout the decade have been quite significant. The church experienced the loss of Edwin Marston, its longest-tenured pastor in 1992.

Marston was followed in 1993 after a short interim period by Charles Smith, the pastor with the shortest tenure in the history of the church. Gains during 1993 were marginal, with a minor upswing in membership of only .2 percent.

The next pastor, Phil Russell, arrived toward the end of 1994. Congregational attendance experienced a modest decline that year of .2 percent. Russell served until mid-1999

---

[151]John Yates, immediate past chairman of deacons of First Baptist Church, interview by author, Town Creek, Ala., 10 November 2000, handwritten notes.

when the church, again, experienced a reduction in membership of .2 percent.

Second, other significant staff changes took place during this period though "the most logical 'blamee' [for a church's decline] is the pastor."[152]   Brett Pitman, the youth minister from 1997-1998, was extremely effective his first year in reaching the teenagers of the community, and as a result the parents joined the church. John Yates attributes the nearly 2 percent increase in resident membership in 1997 to Pitman's efforts.[153]

The modest increase during Pitman's second year is attributed by Yates to Pitman's saturation of the youth market in the small community of Town Creek.[154]   Sunday school

---

[152]Leith Anderson, Jack Hayford, and Ben Patterson Who's In Charge? Standing Up to Leadership Pressures (Sisters, OR: Multnomah, 1993), 41.

[153]Yates, handwritten notes.

[154]Ibid.

director Tommy Smith concurred with this assertion.[155]

Resignation of a Key Volunteer Leader

Charles Simmons, the Sunday school director from 1997-1998, had previously served the Muscle Shoals Baptist Association as Associational Sunday school director. He brought many good ideas to the Sunday school organization of First Baptist Church. These ideas, combined with the significant addition of teenagers and their families during Brett Pitman's tenure, greatly increased average Sunday school attendance during those two years.

This combination, according to both Yates[156] and Smith,[157] accounted for both

---

[155]Tommy Smith, current Sunday school director of First Baptist Church, interview by author, Town Creek, Ala., 25 October 2000, handwritten notes.

Sunday school increases of nearly 9 percent in 1997, and nearly 13 percent in 1998. Simmons, however, resigned in 1998 to join another church as a paid staff member.

Sunday School Reorganization

Several conflicts arose from changes in the Sunday school structure in 1998. The reorganization began in response to suggestions made during a Sunday school clinic.

The pastor (Russell) and Sunday school director (Simmons) strongly endorsed a recommendation by the consultant that the Couples' Class should be canceled. The class was, then, the largest class in the church.

Some class members willingly followed the recommendations of church leadership.

---

[156]Yates, handwritten notes.

[157]Smith, handwritten notes.

They joined separate men and women's classes. The Couples' Class teacher later resigned.

A few members of the class, however, strongly protested the breakup. A small class with a new teacher was allowed to continue because of this objection.

Public Schools

Many new families have joined the church in the last two years (2000-2002). Much of this growth, however, has been offset by transfers to churches in other communities. These transfers have been the result of several families moving their children to other school districts. These children become friends with the children in the new communities; the families, as a result, have moved their church membership to churches in those communities.

OPPORTUNITIES FOR GROWTH

The current pastor began his tenure at First Baptist Church in November 1999. The vision for the church has been to "learn to love Jesus, each other, our community, and our world." The pastor has attempted to follow Dan Reiland's advice, "Share your dream; paint a picture of your vision; be clear and crisp; and describe what the church will look like as it is reshaped."[158]

Movement through each successive level followed the typical process Maxwell identified for adoption. He listed five groups of people with regard to change in an organization.

Maxwell called the first group the "innovators." Innovators "are the originators of new ideas and generally are not acknowledged

---

[158]Reiland, "Mergers and Turnarounds (Part Two)." The Pastor's Coach: Equipping the Leaders of Today's Church, Vol. III, No. 18.

as leaders or policy makers."[159]   They make up approximately 2 percent of the membership of an organization.

The second group he identified was the early adopters. According to Maxwell, "Their opinions are respected in the organization. Although they did not create the idea, they will try to convince others to accept it."[160]   This important group, however, is limited to only 10 percent of the membership of the organization.

The largest group was called the middle adopters. Middle adopters typically include 60 percent of the membership. Maxwell described this group:

> *They will respond to the opinions of others.*
> *Generally they are reasonable in their analysis*
> *of a new idea, but inclined to maintain the*
> *status quo. They can be influenced by the*

---

[159]John Maxwell, Developing the Leader Within You (Nashville: Thomas Nelson, 1993), 64.

[160]Ibid,.64.

positive or negative influencers of the organization.[161]

The remaining 28 percent of the membership consists of the final two groups, the late adopters and laggards. Late adopters, according to Maxwell, "often speak against proposed changes and may never verbally acknowledge acceptance."[162] He continued, "Generally they will adopt it if the majority demonstrates support." Laggards, on the other hand, are committed "to the status quo and the past. Often they try to create division within the organization."[163]

The primary theme of the first year was "learning to love Jesus." Many of the church members responded by making a genuine commitment to give Jesus first priority in their lives.

---

[161]Maxwell, Developing the Leader Within You, 64.

[162]Ibid.

[163]Ibid.

The next year focused upon "learning to love each other." The church members were challenged to love every one of their brothers and sisters in Christ. A smaller, yet significant, group made this decision.

The church has now entered into phase three, "learning to love our community." The primary tool for reaching out to people in the surrounding area has been the Sunday school organization, specifically, the F.A.I.T.H. evangelism strategy. Several church members have adopted this caring mentality. Five teams with a total of seventeen leaders and members visit the community for two-and-one-half hours on Monday evenings.

CHURCH INVOLVEMENT

Church members were involved in two phases of this project. First, an implementation team of key leaders was selected and developed. Second, feedback from the overall congregation was solicited.

Implementation Team

A recent innovation for many churches is the "team ministry" idea. George Barna stated, "Most Protestant churches will not incorporate team leadership into their ministry practices in the foreseeable future."[164] This model of church

---

[164]George Barna, Building Effective Lay Leadership Teams (Ventura, CA: Issachar Resources, 2001), 53.

leadership has several benefits. The model also has some potentially offsetting limitations.

DEFINITION AND DESCRIPTION

A team may be defined as, "a number of persons associated together in work or activity."[165] A team model for a congregation, accordingly, is composed of a group of Christians mutually sharing the ministry responsibilities of a local church.

BENEFITS

People-oriented team ministries are based upon the observation that the members of an

---

[165]Merriam Webster's Collegiate Dictionary, 10th Edition (Springfield, MA: Merriam-Webster, Inc., 1995), 1209.

organization are significant. This rationale has several resultant advantages.

Commitment to Quality

One major advantage of the team approach is an increased commitment to quality. Individual members establish a system of accountability. They thus share the needed responsibility for overall ministry excellence.

Quality is also ensured by the increased likelihood of innovation by team members. James B. Miller, founder and Chief Executive Officer of Miller Business Systems in Arlington, Texas, contended, "Employees can provide the fresh perspective and creativity they gain from interacting with customers every day."[166]

---

[166]James B. Miller, The Corporate Coach (New York: St. Martin's Press, 1993), 82.

Promotion of Spiritual Growth

A second benefit of the team notion is that it promotes the spiritual growth of church members. According to research specialist Charles Barna, "Unless the church challenge[s] the individual to develop his or her alibi-ties, chances [are] good that the individual [will] not grow."[167] These leadership abilities can readily be nurtured and developed in an environment of shared ministerial responsibilities. Barna specified the benefits to the pastor:

> *In team-led churches we discovered that pastors enjoy their vocation more, they stay at their church longer, they are less prone to burnout, and the church is healthier spiritually.*[168]

---

[167]Charles Barna, <u>User Friendly Churches: What Christians Need to Know About the Churches People Love to Go To</u> (Ventura, CA: Regal, 1991), 166.

[168]Barna, <u>Building Effective Lay Leadership Teams</u>, 67.

Endurance Over Time

A third benefit of team ministry model is that the ministry can survive beyond the tenure of the present group. Maxwell asserted, "True success comes only when every generation continues to develop the next generation."[169]

Facilitation of Relationships

A fourth benefit of the team ministry is the facilitation of interpersonal relationships within the church. These associations may help the numerical growth of the congregation. According to Peter Wagner and John L. Gorsuch, "Growing churches put a higher priority on this [fellowship] than nongrowing churches."[170]

---

[169]John Maxwell, Developing the Leaders Around You: How To Help Others Reach Their Full Potential (Nashville: Thomas Nelson, 1995), 198.

[170]C. Peter Wagner and Richard L. Gorsuch, "The Quality Church (Part 1)," Leadership, Winter 1983, 31.

LIMITATIONS

A team ministry also has several inherent limitations. These limitations include the time required for proper application of the ministry, the possibility of missed witnessing opportunities, and the increased potential for power struggles within the leadership core.

Time Factor

The first limitation of the team approach is time invested in the team building process. A leader's personal resources must be devoted to equipping church members to function as a team.

John Maxwell alleged: "Equipping, like nurturing, is an ongoing process. You don't equip a person in a few hours or a day. . . .

Equipping must be tailored to each potential leader."[171]

Missed Opportunities

A second limitation is the potential loss of soul-winning opportunities. The exclusive use of a team ministry method can interfere with church leaders' resources of time and energy. Leaders must demonstrate flexibility in their scheduling to meet prospects from the lost community and cultivate properly those relationships.

Potential for Power Struggles

The team ministry approach presents a greater potential for power struggles among the church leaders. One reason for the increased

---

[171]Maxwell, Developing the Leaders Around You, 84.

capacity for disagreement is that the method is not conducive to the development of a centralized power structure. A single, autocratic leader is required neither to recognize nor consider others' opinions.

Another reason for the increased potential for leader disagreement is related to the first: team ministries generally create a broader base of control. The propensity for conflict within the group is proportionate to the number of trained leaders in the local church.

Team Member Selection

God wants the church to choose the best qualified laborers to begin a new ministry. John Maxwell maintained that church leaders should, "look inside as well as outside the organization to find candidates."[172] Maxwell's plan, which he called the "Five A's," included: assessment of

---

[172]Maxwell, <u>Developing the Leaders Around You</u>, 39.

needs, assets on hand, ability of candidates, attitude of candidates, and accomplishments of candidates.[173]

Three steps in the selection of ministry team candidates can be taken from four of Maxwell's "Five A's." The first step in candidate selection should be an "assessment of needs." Maxwell simply asked the question, "What is needed?"[174] These needs should be written as job descriptions. Each aspect of a particular ministry team function needs to be clearly outlined.

A second, and perhaps more crucial, step can be useful in eliminating those who are reluctant to serve. The question John Maxwell asked in this "attitude of candidates" section was, "Who is willing?"[175] Motivational speaker and author Zig Ziglar agreed with Maxwell regarding the importance of the attitudes of a potential candidate. He stated that: everyone

---

[173]Maxwell, Developing the Leaders Around You, 39.

[174]Ibid.

[175]Ibid.

"share[s] the opinion that [a person's] attitude . . . [in] undertak[ing] a project is the dominant factor in its success."[176]   Ziglar additionally asserted, "A positive attitude will have positive results because attitudes are contagious."[177]

Edwin F. Jenkins concurred, "Most persons agree in the value of one's attitude to help or hinder, to lift or lower one's approach and accomplishment in life's pursuits."[178] Inexperienced workers requiring job training are, consequently, preferable to skilled workers.

The step combined the second and fifth "A's": "assets on hand" and the "accomplishments of candidates."   Two questions asked were "Who are the people already in the organization who are available?" and "Who gets things done?"[179]   Those with

---

[176]Zig Ziglar, See You at the Top (Gretna, LA: Pelican Publishing Company, 1975), 202.

[177]Ibid., 210.

[178]Edwin F. Jenkins, "The Altitude of Church Growth: An Issue of Attitude or Aptitude?" The Alabama Baptist, 30 April 1998, 8.

[179]Maxwell, Developing the Leaders Around You, 39.

previous successful experience in the performance of similar tasks were approached.

Thirteen key leaders were selected and placed in the right positions of responsibility once these questions were answered. This produced several benefits:

> *It maximized natural energy; reduced anxiety, conflict, and tension; increased productivity; increased team spirit, morale, and respect; improved communication; increased confidence; and increased efficiency and competitiveness.[180]*

These thirteen leaders were selected to form an organizational team. The members chosen ranged from lifelong members of First Baptist Church to those who joined in the last year. The only individual member of the team,

---

[180]Bobb Biehl, Stop Setting Goals If You Would Rather Solve Problems (Nashville: Moorings, Random House, 1995), 66.

and first alphabetically, was Gail Boutwell. Gail has been a member of First Baptist for almost three years. She is the teacher of the four and five-year-old Sunday school class, as well as a F.A.I.T.H. (evangelistic strategy) Team Leader, a member of the Adult Choir, a member of the Youth Committee, a member of the Church Ordinance Committee (preparation for the Lord's Supper and assists baptismal candidates), a member of Prayer Team Four (prays for thirty minutes prior to Sunday school on the fourth Sunday of each month), and co-facilitator of the Ladies' Discipleship Training class.

The couples included, first, Andy and Susan Lane. Andy and Susan have been members of First Baptist for almost five years. Andy and Susan are both F.A.I.T.H. Team Learners and members of Prayer Team Three (third Sunday). Andy serves as the church's bi-vocational minister of music, a member (by virtue of position) of the music committee, a Prayer Team member, and as the assistant Sunday school director. Susan serves on a volunteer basis as the Children's Church director.

The second couple selected was Roy and LaVerne Loosier. Roy and LaVerne have been members of First Baptist for more than twenty years and are both F.A.I.T.H. Team Learners. Roy serves as a deacon, teaches a men's Sunday school class (ages thirty-six through fifty-five) and is a member of the Stewardship and Finance Committee. LaVerne teaches the corresponding ladies' Sunday school class.

Roy and Pat Lynch were the third couple chosen to participate on the team. Roy and Pat have been members for less than one year. Roy and Pat are co-teachers of a four-person team for a newly established Young Couples' Sunday school class (ages eighteen through thirty-five). Roy is also an F.A.I.T.H. Team Learner, a member of the adult choir, and a member of the music committee.

The fourth couple selected was Scott and Diane Moore. Scott and Diane have been members of First Baptist for almost three years and are both members of Prayer Team Four. Scott serves as the pastor and, as such, is an ex-officio member of many committees; he is also an F.A.I.T.H. Team Leader.

Diane teaches the fifth and sixth grade Sunday school class, is a member of the Adult Choir, is a co-facilitator for the Ladies' Discipleship Training class, has previously participated as an F.A.I.T.H. Team Learner, and is a member of the Youth Committee.

Roger and Carol Tate were the fifth couple recruited for the team. They are lifelong members of First Baptist and currently serve as co-teachers of the Young Couples' Class (along with Roy and Pat Lynch mentioned above). Roger currently serves as chairman of deacons. He is also the prayer team coordinator, a F.A.I.T.H. Team Leader, and an adult choir member. Carol is the church pianist, a music committee member, and a church ordinance committee member.

The final couple, Willie and Libby Williams, has only been members of First Baptist for six months. Willie and Libby are members of Prayer Team Two and are both F.A.I.T.H. Team Learners. Willie is an ordained preacher and serves on the Benevolence Committee. Libby serves with her daughter, Kim Campbell, as a nursery coordinator.

Team Member Involvement

Expectations for team members were frequently and clearly delineated to ensure the willingness of the team leaders to fulfill the requirements successfully to put the growth factors in place. Doug Fields emphasized this point by stating, "Leaders won't mind hearing your expectations, but they will mind being held accountable for things they haven't been told."[181] Repetition of the requirements for the

---

[181]Doug Fields, Purpose Driven Youth Ministry: Nine Essential Foundations for Healthy Growth (Grand Rapids: Zondervan, 1998), 301.

group members was a crucial step because a breakdown in the communication process could potentially weaken the relationships between them.

The team members were given an initial assignment. Second, they met together for a six-hour training session. Third, they volunteered for various follow-up assignments.

INITIAL ASSIGNMENT

The six couples and one individual were each assigned to attend one of the seven growing rural churches. The assignment was to be completed by the final Sunday in August in order to properly dovetail with the Group Training Session.

The team members collectively attended the morning worship services of seven of the eight growing churches. Each person was given a copy of *Appendix E--QUESTIONNAIRE FOR TEAM MEMBERS* for evaluating the service.

These evaluations were completed and brought to the training session.

GROUP TRAINING SESSIONS

The team members also agreed to attend a six-hour training class (see Appendix F). The sessions were divided into two days and conducted Friday evening and Saturday morning, August 24-25, 2002.

Preparation for the Sessions

The first step in preparation for the group sessions was the selection of the captain. This was an indispensable point. Barna asserted, "Every successful team we observed had a captain in place."[182]

---

[182]Barna, <u>Building Effective Lay Teams</u>, 109.

Candidacy for the position of captain was restricted to team members other than the pastor or other staff member. Professionals were avoided "because the[se] outsider[s] ha[ve] neither a complete understanding of the team's activity and temperament, nor the complete trust of the team members."[183]

The pastor, subsequently, appointed the captain from the lay team members. The reason for this appointment was, "when the team selects its own captain, politics are often at the heart of the selection process."[184]

One style of leadership typically found in team ministry churches is people-oriented. Leaders exercising this style recognize an important fact: "People must not be treated as simply means toward an end--the end or the goals must be established according to the needs of the people."[185] The primary criterion for the selection of the captain, however, was the

---

[183]Barna, <u>Building Effective Lay Teams</u>, 112.

[184]Ibid., 116.

[185]Wagner, <u>Leading Your Church to Growth</u>, 100.

individual's task-orientation. Barna additionally contended that "the Operational Leader is your best bet as a captain, especially since they are process people and the captain's role is a process role."[186] The person selected to serve as captain, Roy Lynch, has consistently displayed an extraordinary ability to keep others performing in a classroom setting.

The role of the captain was explained to the group during the first session Friday night. According to Barna:

> *The effective captain maintains the team's focus on the vision; facilitates positive and productive relationships among team members; identifies opportunities for individual growth; prepares the team to move ahead by acquiring resources; and demonstrates personal leadership productivity.*[187]

[186]Barna, <u>Building Effective Lay Teams</u>, 113.
[187]Ibid., 110-112.

The captain was included in the second preparatory step, planning the group training sessions. Each segment was carefully planned with the objective of focusing on current spiritual victories and future goals to be attained.

Fields stated, "Business issues [were avoided because they can be] discussed and decisions . . . made during the course of any given day."[188] These issues were, therefore, sidestepped due to their ability to deplete motivation from the members of the team.

Friday Evening

The Friday evening session began at 6:00 with a meal supplied by the church. The group members (twelve were present) were then divided into two groups for a time of corporate prayer.

---

[188]Fields, <u>Purpose Driven Youth Ministry</u>, 308.

The two-hour teaching time began at 7:00 p.m. The purpose of this session was to give the team members the necessary background information to participate in the subsequent small group discussions.

Several items were explained. First, the rationale for the choice of participating churches was explained. These churches were examined as to their locations, their growth in average Sunday school attendance and offerings, and their responses to the survey questions.

Second, the team was presented with the statistical analysis of the significance of the responses. The reasons for isolating the four growth factors were enumerated.

Third, each of the four growth factors was explained. These descriptions included both the biblical principles involved and the current findings of various researchers.

Saturday Morning

The Saturday morning session began at 7:00 with a meal, and was led exclusively by the

Team Captain. The team members (twelve were present) were then divided into three groups and assigned a group leader. Each group leader instructed their members to pray for God's leadership for the pursuits of the day.

Next, the entire body was assembled for a large group sharing time. The members were asked to reveal the evidences of the four growth principles observed in the churches they visited.

The groups were then given a threefold assignment: to evaluate the target church regarding the four growth factors; to list the steps they believed would enhance the church's future performance; and to discuss the projected involvement of the team in the process.

The final segment of the morning session was conducted as a large group. The small group leaders explained the ratings of the target church concerning the four growth factors. They also shared recommendations for improvement.

The last phase of the team meeting was twofold. First, the team members reached a consensus regarding several proposed innovations needed for reform.

Second, team members were assigned "specific responsibilities that have meaning and purpose."[189]   The team members personally volunteered to accept the task of motivating the proper persons or existing committees to carry out the proposed innovations.

Team members agreed to a follow-up meeting Saturday, September 28, 2002, at 10:00 a.m. The session was concluded with prayer.

The Proposed Innovations

The team members proposed projects for three of the four growth principles. The three principles included God's presence in the service, the friendliness of the members, and the doctrinal position of the church; team members,

---

[189]Fields, Purpose Driven Youth Ministry, 298.

however, made no recommendation for the pastor and preaching.

GOD'S PRESENCE

Four innovations were proposed concerning the presence of God. All centered on the enrichment of corporate prayer life.

Teachers' Prayer Meeting

First, the team proposed a weekly prayer meeting for Sunday school teachers. This meeting would take place at 9:30 a.m., twenty minutes before the beginning of classes. The teachers would pray for their students, each other, the newly formed Young Couples' Class, and the church services for the day.

Roy Lynch, the team captain, proposed an additional prayer time during the team meeting on Saturday, October 5, 2002. He suggested

Teachers' Meetings on Wednesday evenings could be concluded at the altar for a time of prayer.

Lynch assumed the responsibility of follow-up for this project. He reported to the congregation that this project is still in the planning stage.

Weekday Prayer Room

Second, the team proposed the establishment of a weekday prayer room. This room would need to be accessible for anyone wishing to pray (without leaving the entire church open to outsiders), have restroom facilities, and be separately climate-controlled. The team favored the use of an auxiliary building located at the Northeast corner of the church property.

The team captain also accepted the obligation for this task. Lynch reported his investigation of the prayer room ministry in a nearby church in Florence, Alabama.

Calvary Fellowship has two one-hour prayer meetings every weekday. The sessions are held at 5:30 a.m. and 7:00 p.m. The room is staffed for each session by a volunteer with the responsibility of unlocking the room, meeting with those who wish to pray, and the locking the room at the end of the service.

Lynch also recommended a small, informal setting for the room. The rationale for his suggestion was to facilitate the communication of special prayer needs.

Scott Moore (the pastor) additionally proposed the physical layout for the prayer room. The room could be divided according to the pattern established by Perry Hancock, Broadmoor Professor of Discipleship at New Orleans Baptist Theological Seminary. The Intercessory Prayer Center at New Orleans has been "designed with five stations for prayer."[190]

---

[190]Perry Hancock, "Intercessory Prayer Center," <u>NOBTS Website</u> (New Orleans: New Orleans Baptist Theological Seminary, 2002).

The students and faculty are encouraged to pray for the seminary, the city of New Orleans, the state of Louisiana, and the North American and the International Mission Board of the Southern Baptist Convention.

The concepts for four of the five stations at First Baptist could be taken from the New Testament book of the Revelation. Four "in the Spirit" passages are found in the book: Revelation 1:10, 4:2, 17:3, and 21:10.

The first station, confession, is based upon Revelation 1:10. The Apostle John wrote, "What thou seest, write in a book, and send it unto the seven churches." The churches each had a particular sin (or implied sin) for which they were being corrected. Each prayer session could begin with confession of both personal and corporate sin.

A second station could be devoted to praise. John stated in Revelation 4:2, "and, behold, a throne was set in heaven, and one sat on the throne." The throne room of Heaven, with God Himself on the throne, elicits the praise of anyone who is invited there. People praying would enter into a time of praise for the One who is worthy of praise.

A third station is the place of the request, or petition, of the believer. John declared in Revelation 17:3a, "So he carried me away in the spirit into the wilderness." This wilderness could be perceived as the place where spiritual needs are presented. Time at this station could be a time of sharing personal needs with the Heavenly Father.

The fourth station becomes the place of blessing. John further stated in Revelation 21:10, "And he carried me away in the spirit to a great and high mountain, and showed me that great city, the holy Jerusalem, descending out of heaven from God." The greatest blessing believers will ever know is that of being forever united with their Bridegroom, Jesus Christ, in the new home the Heavenly Father has created for them.

The final station would be dedicated to worship. Worship is simply silence and reverence before God. This station of prayer is the place of rest in the presence of the Lord.

Monthly Prayer Letter

The third proposed innovation was the development of a monthly prayer letter for members of the existing Prayer Teams. The prayer letter could include updates for needs throughout the church family, as well as the inclusion of an "answered prayer" section. The letter could also be utilized as a recruitment tool for new Prayer Team members. The team captain reported this suggestion was also in the planning stage.

FRIENDLINESS

Six ideas were proposed by team members to increase the friendliness of the membership. One idea would require the formation of a new group of church members designated as "greeters." The greeters will, as their name infers, greet people before and after the worship services. They will also be responsible for directing guests to Sunday school classes, nursery facilities, rest rooms, and the auditorium. Roy Loosier and Libby Williams accepted the responsibility of supervising these efforts.

Loosier and Williams subsequently circulated an enrollment form in the youth and adult Sunday school classes enlisting the assistance of members at one of three times: before Sunday school, after Sunday school, and after church. They will continue to enlist workers and then recommend a chairperson to coordinate the efforts when the group is established.

Another idea required an organizational step for an existing organization, the appointment of a chairman of the Usher Committee. Carol Tate volunteered to oversee this endeavor.

The Committee previously had no chairman; the Nominating Committee, accordingly, selected a candidate from the list of those serving and presented his name for approval from the entire church. Hoover Reding is now serving as chairman. He currently schedules the ushers for each service, and is planning a training event.

The church is beginning to reach young families through the efforts of the F.A.I.T.H. Evangelism Strategy and the establishment of the Young Couples' Sunday school Class. Many of these couples have expressed an interest in attending Discipleship Training, Sunday evening services, and Wednesday evening prayer meetings. A third idea proposed by the team members, therefore, focused upon needed improvements in childcare.

Additional workers will be needed to serve during these services. Gail Boutwell and Susan Lane are serving in this recruitment capacity.

An appeal for more workers was made during the two worship services on Sunday, October 6, 2002. The single nursery room will be divided into separate babies' and toddlers' rooms.

The nursery worker is, following the guest and the usher, the most important person in a worship service. Maxwell contended that:

> *Nursery workers are vital because young parents will select a church   more on the nursery care than on the doctrinal statements of the congregation. Nursery workers give assurance to the parents that their child will be cared for.* [191]

Susan Lane also proposed the addition of an AWANA program for children ages four through sixth grade. AWANA "is a nondenominational ministry that assists churches in reaching children and teenagers

---

[191]John C. Maxwell, <u>Ushers and Greeters</u> (El Cajon, CA: INJOY Ministries, 1991), 1-5.

with the gospel of Jesus Christ and training them to serve Him."[192]

Lane advised both the team members and the church members of the availability of an in-house training session offered by the Decatur Baptist Church. Those interested were encouraged to attend.

Lane also suggested the purchase of teaching materials from the David C. Cook Company for use during Sunday evening services. She mentioned the information is user-friendly, and would thus require little planning on the part of workers.

Three church members added some thoughts regarding the Children's Ministries of the church. One member suggested the formation of a puppet ministry. Another participant expanded the idea to involve youth in puppet performances during Sunday evening services. A third respondent suggested offering an instructional program for local students. This

---

[192]AWANA Clubs International. <u>AWANA: Who We Are, What We Do</u> (Streamwood, IL: AWANA Website Online), 2002.

person also recommended a sponsorship program for children similar to the "Big Brothers" or "Big Sisters" organizations.

A fourth team member recommendation would require some building improvements. Andy Lane expressed interest in this project. He stated that the church's Buildings and Grounds Committee had attended four meetings during the month of September 2002.

The committee, with the endorsement of the deacons, will make several recommendations during an upcoming business meeting. They will propose several projects at little or no cost to the church, including: cleaning the carpet throughout the buildings, painting the classrooms (class members would provide paint and labor), landscaping, and cleaning the steeple.

The committee also plans to propose the establishment of a Building Fund. The fund will be used for major repairs needed for the existing facilities. The committee also advocated a ten-year time frame for the construction of a new building.

Members of the committee also made several suggestions regarding the fund. They recommended the fund be kept in a separate checking account from the existing general fund account. No recommendations for fund usage will be accepted directly from the floor of business meetings; all requests must be approved by the Building and Grounds Committee and then presented to the church for approval.

The Building Fund will be established through two primary sources. First, two major offerings will be taken each year: the first Sunday in May and the fourth Sunday in October. Second, church members will be given the opportunity to make either a one-time donation or to make a monthly pledge toward the fund.

Committee members suggested that these gifts be given in addition to the ongoing tithes of the constituents. This suggestion will minimize the possibility of the reduction in gifts to the general fund previously experienced during collection of other special offerings.

The fifth idea in this category would encourage the Social Committee to conduct more fellowship activities after Sunday morning services. Team members interested in this project were Diane Moore and Pat Lynch.

Lynch and Moore proposed several social activities. First, they made several suggestions for the four fifth Sundays each year: a church-wide meal after the morning service, special music, guest and member soloists, a concert for the youth, and a short sermon.

Second, they recommended that Sunday school class members sponsor families with food for Thanksgiving, children's gifts for Christmas, and school supplies at the beginning of each school year. These families will be identified through benevolence requests, the van ministry, and AWANA classes.

Third, Lynch and Moore made several recommendations for small group gatherings.

These suggestions included, first, an annual Mother-Daughter Banquet. Second, they recommended a fellowship time for Sunday school teachers. Lynch and Moore asserted the social needs of this group have been overlooked in the past. Third, Lynch and Moore suggested a church-wide Family Day. They recommended meeting at a local park, bringing food for a picnic, and offering games for all ages.

Moore (the pastor) subsequently added the sixth idea of a second morning worship service. The introduction of multiple services will demonstrate concern for the needs of people.

Merchants in the marketplace have learned that business hours should be set at the customer's convenience. People will gravitate to those businesses that are open when they want to shop. The churches that are "open for business" when people are ready to go will have, obviously, more "customers" than those who do not.

James Emery White, the senior pastor of the Mecklenburg Community Church in Charlotte, North Carolina, stated, "Most persons do not want their day disrupted to the degree that a service ending at noon has the tendency to accomplish."[193] Jim McCoy, the former minister of music in a church that has offered multiple morning worship services for years, concurred: "We were able to reach some people who were looking for a church that offered an early service."[194]

Another advantage of the second worship service is the difference in size of the two gatherings. One service will have more in attendance than the other. Wood maintained, "[This differential gives] people who prefer smaller numbers [the] opportunity [to worship with a smaller group]. Some folks [seem to] prefer the smaller church atmosphere."[195]

---

[193]James Emery White, Opening the Front Door: Worship and Church Growth (Nashville: Convention Press, 1992), 102.

[194]W. Scott Moore, "Multiple Morning Worship Service Questionnaire," 1.

[195]Ibid.

Two basic traffic flow problems, however, will result from offering a new worship service. One such matter will be the flow of people within the church facility. Major consideration should be given to the entrance hall. Architect Ray Bowman suggested:

> *The construction of a fellowship foyer. . . . [This foyer] is large enough to give worshipers leaving one service and those arriving for the next enough room to visit with each other and welcome visitors without blocking traffic.*[196]

Another design consideration that can aid in people management is greater accessibility to areas of potentially high traffic. Rooms such as the nursery and greeting stations should be placed in convenient locations. They should be near the sanctuary with hallways large enough

---

[196]Ray Bowman and Eddy Hall, When Not to Build: An Architect's Unconventional Wisdom for the Growing Church (Grand Rapids: Baker, 1992), 123.

to accommodate the volume of people during the transition between services.

The other traffic flow problem is the movement into, and out of, the parking lots. People coming to the late service must find a parking place or they will develop an unfavorable opinion regarding the early service. Parking is such a crucial matter that Kennon L. Callahan, founder and senior consultant of the National Institute for Church Planting and Consultation, stated:

> *Some researchers suggest that it is important for a   church to have approximately 20 percent of its parking area empty on a given Sunday so that the large hidden sign that is hung out front says "come on in; there is room in the inn for you."*[197]

---

[197]Kennon L. Callahan, Twelve Keys to an Effective Church: Strategic Planning for Mission (San Francisco, CA: HarperSanFrancisco, Harper Collins, 1983), 89.

DOCTRINAL POSITION

Third, two ideas were advanced to promote the clarification of the doctrinal position of the church. The pastor (Scott Moore) and Willie Williams will be responsible for the formation of this new class.

A proposed doctrinal class could be introduced during the Sunday school hour for guests and new members. January 2003 was suggested as the target date for starting the new class.

The team recommended the revision of the existing Discipleship Training schedule to include a similar elective for the present membership. Team member Roger Tate volunteered to assist the Discipleship Training director (his son, Casey) in both establishing and promoting this class.

Tate (Roger) approached two former teachers of a disbanded Discipleship Training class about the possibility of beginning this course; they declined. Tate, therefore, recommended we delay this proposal until teachers can be secured.

Follow-up meeting

The follow-up meeting was rescheduled and conducted on Saturday, October 5, 2002, at 6:00 p.m. The pastor and six additional team members took part in the conference.

Each participant was given a form with the alphabetical listing of Rainer's thirteen primary growth factors. They were instructed to rank the factors from one to four. All six respondents listed the four correct growth factors. Five of the six participants also listed them in proper order.

Church Member Involvement

The pastor preached four separate Sunday evening messages throughout the month of August 2002 to address the growth principles uncovered individually by the project (see Appendix G). The sermons were preached in reverse order as follows: Sermon Four--Sunday, August 4, 2002; Sermon Three--Sunday, August 11, 2002; Sermon Two--Sunday, August 18, 2002; and Sermon One--Sunday, August 25, 2002.

The Sunday evening service, October 7, 2002, was dedicated to an open forum "town meeting." Forty-four members and guests participated in the service. The meeting consisted of three steps. First, each participant was given two forms. Second, the team captain informed the group regarding team member recommendations for future growth projects. Third, the participants were polled for suggestions for future improvements.

The first form distributed was the alphabetical listing of Rainer's thirteen primary growth factors previously given to the team members. The instructions on top of the form stated: "Church growth expert Thom Rainer listed thirteen primary growth factors. Rank the top four factors for rural churches, in order, from one to four." The purpose of the form was to discover the effectiveness of the pastor's communication of the factors from the pulpit.

Seventy-five percent (thirty-three people) of the participants properly identified "God's presence/atmosphere in the church" as the number one response. The response was significant, as this factor has been repeatedly emphasized.

Thirty-six percent of this subgroup properly listed all four factors in order. An additional 10 percent listed the top two factors in order.

Ten percent of forty-four participants listed three of the top four in the wrong order. Two percent listed two of the top four incorrectly. Four percent listed only one of the top four factors in their responses. Four percent of the respondents did not understand the directions, as they attempted to rate all thirteen responses.

The second form distributed was a variation of Appendix E--QUESTIONNAIRE FOR TEAM MEMBERS. The forty-four participants rated the First Baptist Church of Town Creek regarding the four growth factors. They were also given the opportunity to add their personal comments for each factor.

GOD'S PRESENCE

Seventy-eight percent of the respondents rated the presence of God/atmosphere of the church at either level three or level four: moderately or greatly significant. Twenty-three percent suggested that this growth factor was only "mildly significant" in the worship services.

No one answered with the "insignificant" response.

The consensus was that God's presence has been strongly experienced in the services. The following illustration showed the importance of placing the greatest emphasis upon this top priority:

> *Charles Schwab, then president of Bethlehem Steel, brought in management consultant Ivy Lee for one primary need: help the president discover how to get more done in the same amount of time. Mr. Lee took a three-by-five card out of his pocket and gave it to Mr. Schwab. "I want you to write down the things that need to be done tomorrow, in the order of their real importance. When you come in to work tomorrow, I want you to work on number one until it is completed. At the end of the day, write a new list. Try this system as long as you like, then have your*

staff try it. Evaluate this activity, and send me a check for what you think it's worth."[198]

Rainer concluded: "In a few weeks Mr. Schwab sent Mr. Lee a check for $25,000! Such may be the value of establishing your priorities!"[199]

One participant commented, "God's presence has been in our services a lot lately."[200] A second member agreed, "We're moving in the right direction."[201] A third made reference to recent Teachers' Meetings, "Number three on Wednesday night. [We] need the Spirit in all the services."[202] A fourth participant suggested the presence of God is "increasing every week; the

---

[198]Carl F. George and Robert E. Logan, Leading And Managing Your Church (Old Tappan, NJ: Fleming H. Revell, 1987), 45.

[199]Thom S. Rainer, Eating the Elephant: Bite-Sized Steps To Achieve Long-Term Growth In Your Church (Nashville: Broadman and Holman, 1994), 187.

[200]Gail South, Open Forum Meeting, 7 October 2002, Town Creek, AL. Handwritten notes.

[201]Ibid.

[202]Ibid.

more people that participate in praise [and worship], the better it is."[203]   A fifth participant stated, "We do [experience God's presence] a whole lot!"[204]   A sixth simply stated, "[It's] getting better every week."[205]   A seventh respondent said, "God has most definitely been in this church."[206]

Some disagreed with the above statements.   Three participants courteously expressed their opposition.   One stated, "[It] could be better."[207]   Another said, "We can always do better."[208]   The third said, "We need more prayer."[209]

Three additional respondents were more cautious.   One asserted, "Sometimes [the] Spirit [is] not good."[210]   Another stated, "[It] seems

[203]South, Open Forum Meeting, Handwritten notes.

[204]Ibid.

[205]Ibid.

[206]Ibid.

[207]Ibid.

[208]Ibid.

[209]Ibid.

[210]Ibid.

dry at times."[211] The third warned, "I just feel sometimes like there [are] some negative forces working against the people who want to see God come down."[212]

One of the teenagers proposed a revival service to target the youth in the Town Creek and neighboring communities. She suggested the church's former minister of youth as the evangelist.

An adult member proposed a church-wide revival. She expressed the need occasionally to conduct services other than the usual Sunday and Wednesday gatherings.

FRIENDLINESS

The second growth factor received a significantly lower evaluation. Sixty-six percent

---

[211]South, Open Forum Meeting, Handwritten notes.
[212]Ibid.

of the participants ranked First Baptist Church at the three and four levels of significance.

The respondents rated the element of friendliness the lowest of the four growth factors. The church members, consequently, need to endeavor to become more sociable toward guests and other members.

Participant responses ranged from favorable to extremely unfavorable. Favorable responses included, "extremely friendly," "very friendly," "I like when we shake hands," and "We are improving."[213]

Other participants gave ambiguous reviews. They stated, "Always room for growth," "could be better," "it's selective," "some [people are] friendly, but not all," and "we have some very friendly [people], but some [others are] sour."[214]

The last group responded negatively. Two participants addressed the perceived

---

[213]South, Open Forum Meeting, Handwritten notes.
[214]Ibid.

malevolence of some members, "Many people talk or laugh at others, [and hold] grudges," and "Many members have 'grudges' against others."[215] Another said, "We need to improve greatly [in] this [area]." A fourth stated, "[Some of the members are] a little stuffy."[216]

Two additional respondents pointed out specific groups of people they believed were adversely affecting the friendliness of the church. They stated, "[The] greeters could improve," and "There are still some of our older members who are not very friendly."[217]

Several ideas were proposed during the open forum meeting on Sunday, October 6, 2002. A guest mentioned the "Through Every Door" campaign conducted by a Southern Baptist church in a neighboring community. Subsequent research revealed:

---

[215]South, Open Forum Meeting, Handwritten notes.

[216]Ibid.

[217]Ibid.

> *The program is part of a larger statewide
> initiative. Participants will be asked to
> conduct surveys of residents in
> neighborhood[s], the results of which will help
> local churches more effectively meet needs in
> their communities.*[218]

A member recommended the formation of a Crisis Support Group. This ministry would be made available to meet the needs of church members and nonmembers in the Town Creek community.

Other members advocated church involvement in mission trips. One teenager expressed an interest in taking part in a mission construction project.

Several members (and one guest) made suggestions for services with special themes. One member mentioned a Youth Day: a worship service involving various teenagers in teaching

---

[218]James Dotson, "Crossover Presents Varied Opportunities for Volunteers to Share Faith in Orlando" Baptist Press (Nashville: Baptist Press, 22 February 2000).

the classes, serving as ushers, taking the offering, singing in the choir, leading the music, playing the musical instruments, and preaching.

Two participants recommended honoring the Senior Adult members of the church. One recommended conducting a Senior Adult worship service. The other participant proposed a Senior Adult Banquet: a special annual meal week to pay tribute to senior church members.

A fourth participant recommended that the church celebrate a Men's Day. The men would lead in all the Sunday school classes and be invited to participate in a Men's Choir.

A fifth member suggested that the church sponsor a Women's Retreat. The event would be held at First Baptist Church; ladies from the other churches in the area would be invited to attend.

A sixth member proposed a "Dorcas Day." She commented that the event is named after Dorcas, a disciple mentioned in Acts 9:39: "and all the widows stood by him weeping, and shewing the coats and garments which Dorcas made, while she was with them." *Dorcas Day*, therefore, would be an opportunity for church members to donate clothing they would normally have sold in a yard sale to the church. The clothing could then be distributed to needy families in the community.

A seventh person (a nonmember) suggested a "Family and Friend Day." Members would be encouraged to invite their family members, neighbors, and friends to a special Sunday morning worship service. The church previously observed a Friend Day in 1999, with more than two hundred in attendance.

DOCTRINAL POSITION

The participants gave this response the highest rating of the four growth factors. They overwhelmingly agreed that the church modeled doctrinal integrity. Eighty-four percent of the respondents voted in the three and four ranges of significance. Seven percent rated this factor at level one: insignificant or unimportant in its impact upon the church.

Five members commented on this growth factor. One said, "We are show[n] every Sunday where we stand and where we should be."[219] The second asserted, "[We have a] good vision."[220] The third responded: "Our doctrine is complete. We just don't do what we believe."[221] The fourth commented, "[Doctrinal truths] need to be expressed more." The fifth contended, "[The position of the church] could be better."[222]

PASTOR AND PREACHING

Eighty-one percent of the participants believed the pastor and his preaching are

---

[219]South, Open Forum Meeting, Handwritten notes.

[220]Ibid.

[221]Ibid.

[222]South, Open Forum Meeting.

functioning at either the three or four levels. A modest 2 percent of the respondents believed this growth factor was insignificant.

The team members made no recommendations for the improvement of this growth factor. Only one participant responded during the open forum meeting by verbalizing the need to pray for the pastor. The reason for the limited involvement may have been a lack of anonymity.

A solution for this dilemma was the distribution of an unsigned questionnaire presented to church members at the October 2, 2002, meeting. Positive comments recognized several items. One respondent stated, "The pastor is much improved in his preaching over the past two years."[223] Another participant made the personal comment, "When it seems we all need to be cherished a little, God seems to give you a heart for the right things to say."[224]

---

[223]South, Open Forum Meeting, Handwritten notes.
[224]Ibid.

One member expressed appreciation for the Sunday morning sermon outlines contained in the bulletins.

Members of the congregation gave mixed reviews of the pastor's sense of humor. One stated, "He has a good [sense of] humor, which is refreshing."[225] Two others countered, "need less jokes/funny stuff," and "less joking.[226]"

Criticisms were both general and specific. The first member stated, "[The pastor] could do better."[227]

The second and third responses were more candid. One participant stated, "[The pastor is] too critical."[228]

The other respondent stated, "Some messages are confusing; sermons written weeks or longer ahead of time seem [more likely] to point out individuals."[229] The first statement is

---

[225]South, Open Forum Meeting, Handwritten notes

[226]Ibid.

[227]Ibid.

[228]Ibid.

[229]Ibid.

accurate because some sermon themes are more elementary than others. The next two statements were based upon two false assumptions: that the pastor writes messages several weeks in advance and that he intentionally focuses upon one individual in the messages.

CONCLUSION

This writer has observed, throughout the duration of this study, many valuable church growth principles applicable to churches of all sizes. Research in the specific field of rural church growth has been, however, very limited. The situation is unfortunate because, as was mentioned earlier, "most of the sixteen million Southern Baptists were classified in a news article as living in either suburban, small town, or rural areas."[230] The project, therefore, was a mixture of both investigation and application.

The project was evaluated regarding the stated objectives. The following objectives were accomplished. First, the four primary rural church growth principles were isolated and studied.

---

[230]Julia Leiblich, "Southern Baptist President Urges Outreach" <u>Athens Daily News</u> (Athens, GA: Online Athens) 16 June 1999.

Second, a team of thirteen individuals was selected. These team members visited seven of the eight growing churches, completed an evaluation form, and attended a six-hour training class. They subsequently attended a separate follow-up meeting to discuss progress toward stated goals.

Third, the congregation was involved. Four Sunday evening messages were used both to illustrate and explain the four growth factors. Individual and committee tasks were delegated and two new committees were proposed.

Fourth, the results were reported to the church. Reactions were solicited from those directly involved in the project (the team members). Those activities that have contributed to church growth will be continued.

The entire process took approximately six months. It began in March 2002 with the study of the seven growing Southern Baptist churches and concluded with the open forum meeting on Sunday, October 6, 2002.

The project successfully involved many participants. The writer, team members, and church members gained several insights.

What the Writer Learned

The writer learned much about the distinctiveness of the rural church. First, he learned several factors do *not* help in the growth of a rural church. The respondents gave high marks to the importance of Children's and Youth Ministries. Application of statistical techniques, however, placed this discipline below the necessary threshold to be considered for this project.

Three rejected factors were obvious to this writer: lay leadership, a strong sense of "community," the location of the churches, and population growth. Most rural churches in Town Creek, Alabama, and the surrounding areas are pastor-centered; lay leadership in these churches has been, traditionally, an undeveloped resource.

The second and third factors were related. The location of the churches was insignificant due to a lack of population growth. The churches studied have experienced either small growth or decline in their communities.

Several responses, however, were unanticipated. The current debate concerning worship styles is apparently immaterial to the growth of a rural church. This was a beneficial response because, according to Rainer, "For many, the worship service is, in a very deep and emotional way, the church."[231]

The Sunday school organization was given very little credit in the growth of the churches polled in the survey. This writer strongly disagreed with those findings, however, and is planning to continue endorsing this institution. Hemphill and Jones stated, "Church growth is a process and not an event. Church

---

[231]Thom Rainer, <u>Effective Evangelistic Churches</u> (Nashville: Broadman and Holman, 1996), 99.

growth may use events, but no one or two events will sustain growth." They further maintained, "Sunday school by its very nature is a process and not an event."[232]

The respondents also ranked evangelistic programs or strategies as unimportant. Some of the churches polled either may have not used these methods or considered them ineffective in the retention of visitors.

Members of First Baptist Church of Town Creek (the target church), to the contrary, have found F.A.I.T.H. to be a highly effective means of reaching out to the community. They have used this strategy for evangelism, visiting guests and absentees, and for meeting various ministry needs. Welch stated that::

> *The purpose of the program was to motivate the readers and their churches to experience personally and collectively an explosion in*

[232]Ken Hemphill and R. Wayne Jones, Growing an Evangelistic Sunday School (Nashville: Broadman, 1989), 59-60.

> *growth individually and churchwide by combining Sunday school and evangelism.*[233]

A sense of "community" was also rejected by the respondents. This component has made a minor contribution to the maintenance and growth of the target and other nearby churches.

An unanticipated side benefit of this research was the discovery of the correlation between the numerical growth and the financial growth of the seven churches. The total membership for all seven churches increased by 59 percent. The churches accordingly experienced a total increase in offerings of 48 percent. Rural church growth, therefore, makes financial resources available for the associated needs of additional staff and building projects.

Only one recommendation was made during the open forum meeting concerning the pastor and preaching. The pastor subsequently designed several self-improvement projects.

---

[233]Bobby H. Welch, <u>Evangelism Through the Sunday School: A Journey of FAITH</u> (Nashville: Lifeway Press, 1999), p. 25.

Each project was intended to strengthen the pastor personally in the areas of the presence of God (prayer life), friendliness, and/or doctrinal position. John Maxwell stated: "Leadership doesn't develop in a day. It takes a lifetime."[234]

The pastor also needs an accountability partner. The selection process for this colleague will require much prayer but will assist in effective implementation of the personal growth plans.

PRESENCE OF GOD

The pastor currently spends from thirty minutes to one hour each morning in prayer and Bible study. This discipline has recently been improved through a concept explained by Buddy Owens at a recent "Promise Keepers" Conference in Nashville, Tennessee, and

---

[234]John Maxwell, The 21 Irrefutable Laws of Leadership: Follow Them and People Will Follow You (Nashville: Thomas Nelson, 1998), 31.

described in his book. Owens has worked with Maranatha! Music for fifteen years, was the General Editor of the N.I.V. Worship Bible, and is a national conference speaker for various organizations.

Owens commented that most people regard prayer and Bible study as separate disciplines. They either pray first and then read their Bibles, or study their Bibles first and then pray.

He suggested the alternative of "read[ing] the Bible meditatively."[235] He utilized the word picture of a scenic drive through the mountains to describe the process. The drive began with filling the gas tank, or "ask[ing] God to fill you afresh with his Holy Spirit."[236]

The second step involved choosing the "road." This meant to:

---

[235]Buddy Owens, The Way of a Worshiper: Discover the Secret of Friendship with God (San Clemente, CA: Maranatha Publishing, 2002), 123.

[236]Ibid., 125.

Select your passage. It may be an old favorite you've read many times. It may even be the passage you read yesterday. Or it may be a new "road" you've never explored before.[237]

The third step was to "slow down and take in the beauty of your surroundings."[238] Owens suggested several questions should be answered at this point in the journey: "What else is going on in the surrounding verses? What are you discovering about God's nature in the text? What are you seeing that you may not have seen before?"[239]

Fourth, the person praying needed to "pull over at a scenic viewpoint."[240] This simply requires the person to focus on one or more phrases or verses within the passage, stress various words within the phrases or verses, and then put the words in their own language.

---

[237]Owens, The Way of a Worshiper, (San Clemente,., 126.

[238]Ibid.

[239]Ibid.

[240]Ibid., 127.

The fifth step was to "take a picture of yourself before you move on."[241] God's Word, described as a "mirror," will expose the worshiper's true spiritual condition.

The final step involved "send[ing] home a postcard. This is your prayer."[242] Owens described this concluding step as:

> *God is leading me in prayer. He is directing the conversation. By praying through the Scriptures, I am now praying God's thoughts back to God. I am, in a very real sense, agreeing with God in prayer.*[243]

The pastor should also lead the church in improvement of the corporate prayer life. Two prayer emphases in the past could become traditional events. First, church members were involved in "Ten Days of Prayer" in the year 2000. These ten days were a celebration of the

---

[241]Owens, The Way of a Worshiper, 129.

[242]Ibid., 130.

[243]Ibid.

time the early church spent in united prayer prior to the outpouring of God's presence and power on the day of Pentecost. Meetings were held on various days in either the church auditorium or individual members' homes.

Second, the church recently participated in four days of prayer. Andy Lane suggested the need for corporate humility in order to reach the community with the gospel. The meetings were conducted in the auditorium and in the homes of various participants.

FRIENDLINESS

Several activities were considered useful for improvement in the pastor's capacity for friendliness. First, the pastor is not currently teaching a Sunday school class. He has endorsed the Sunday school organization through regular attendance in the *Willing Workers'* class (couples age thirty-six through fifty-five). He could, however, implement the policy that he and the minister of music (the minister of youth currently teaches a class) schedule visits to a different department each week until all classes have been visited.

Second, the pastor could begin the doctrinal Sunday school class, or pastor's class (see innovation nine above). This would make the pastor more accessible to a small group of people.

A third activity would require the pastor to arrive in the auditorium before the morning service. This would allow more time to socialize with the members and guests.

A fourth assignment could be accomplished during the existing Wednesday night fellowship suppers. The pastor, minister of music, and youth minister will intentionally sit on a rotating basis with different clusters of people each night. The existing groups include: the youth, young families and median adults, and the senior adults.

The final activity would be exercised during the prayer meeting, and is similar to the second exercise. A typical service begins with attendees sharing prayer requests with the group. The pastor leads a short Bible study followed by a small group prayer time. The two staff members in attendance, the pastor and minister of music, could be assigned to rotate participation between groups.

DOCTRINAL POSITION

The pastor could strengthen the doctrinal position of the church in two ways. First, he could preach more doctrinal messages. The Sunday night services would be an ideal time to address various tenets of the Christian faith.

A second activity could be conducted during the Bible study segment of the Wednesday evening service. This project could include teaching such topics as the upcoming January Bible study or The Baptist Faith and Message.

What the Team Members Learned

The team members also gained several important insights. First, they discovered the value of participation in a team venture. Much more can be accomplished in the local church by the efforts of a group than by the individual pastor. Many of the participants were relatively new members of the target church. Lyle E. Schaller stated:

> *Most long-established churches resemble a closed circle. Most of the resources are allocated to meeting the needs of the members already within that circle. This includes the priorities on the pastor's time and energy, the use of the building, the ministry of music, the priorities in the spending of money, and the use of the time contributed by volunteers.*[244]

[244]Lyle E. Schaller, "Will the Circle Be Broken?" Leadership Journal, Summer 1998, vol. XIX, no. 3, 31.

Schaller further suggested that this "closed circle" could be opened up "by creating new and attractive entry points for newcomers."[245] These team members were thus introduced into the organization in a leadership capacity.

Second, team members recognized the effort needed to grow a rural church. Rural congregations do not have an abundance of unsolicited guests in their weekly services. These churches must, therefore, become both meticulous in their outreach and distinctive in the reception of their guests.

Third, the participants personally observed the application of the four factors in the seven growing rural churches they visited. The insights they gained strongly influenced the formulation of the action plans they later proposed for the target church.

Fourth, team members were polled as a group for suggestions to implement the growth factors into the structure of the target church.

---

[245]Schaller, "Will the Circle Be Broken?" 31.

Each team member volunteered to supervise the implementation of one or more desired changes in the target church.

How the Project Will Impact the Church

The overall membership of First Baptist Church will be involved in three future facets of the project. First, members of various committees listed in the team members' recommendations will be consulted and asked to administer the necessary changes. These groups will include the following committees: the Building and Grounds Committee, the Nominating Committee, the Prayer Teams Committee, the Social Committee, and the Usher Committee.

Second, two new committees will be proposed: the greeters and the Sunday school teachers' prayer group. These new entities will require the participation of additional people.

Third, some proposed innovations will require the involvement of several key individuals in the church. The Discipleship Training director, the Sunday school director, and the nursery coordinator would all need to be consulted regarding the proposed changes.

Reiland's admonition will guide the implementation of the various ideas proposed by the team members and church members. He stated:

> *Keep the list short. Be tough in the decision-making process, but focus your effort and energy on the few things that must change. You don't have the time or the resources to chase things that don't matter. Too many churches get lost in surface issues rather than those that make a difference.*[246]

---

[246]Reiland, "Mergers and Turnarounds (Part Two)." <u>The Pastor's Coach: Equipping the Leaders of Today's Church</u>, Vol. III, No. 18.

How the Project Could Impact Other Churches

Additional research is needed, therefore, to assist rural Southern Baptist churches in reaching their communities with the gospel of Christ. Pastors and other leaders of churches could benefit from an understanding of the dynamics of the growth factors in their distinctive congregational settings.

The effectiveness of these principles as instruments for church development has already been established by the seven growing congregations. The applicability of the standards to other churches will be observed in the future growth patterns of First Baptist Church of Town Creek, Alabama.

The same criteria used to identify the seven growing churches will be applied to the target church. Average Sunday school attendance must experience a DGR of at least 50 percent in order to warrant the continuation of this undertaking.

The DGR, as previously mentioned, can be calculated for intervals of less than ten years. This writer, therefore, will periodically examine these figures with reference to the target church for the next several months and years.

Reiland's statement regarding growth loosely established an ideal time line, "While there is no formula, the initial phases can easily take 18 months, with the first signs of success not becoming obvious for 36 months."[247] The ideas gleaned from this project will subsequently be considered transferrable if and when the minimum DGR of 50 percent is achieved.

The growth principles may also be made available in the future to rural churches in other denominations. The ultimate findings of this study could, therefore, be rewritten by this author and submitted to a publishing house for popular distribution.

---

[247]Reiland, "Mergers and Turnarounds (Part Two)."

APPENDICES

Appendix A--GROWTH SURVEY

Please rate the following factors according to their impact upon the growth of your church:

Fill in your response to the right of each question below:

1=none   2=minor   3=moderate   4=major

1. Population growth--recent development of your community ___

2. Evangelistic programs/strategies ___

3. Lay leadership--deacons, teachers, etc. ___

4. Children's/Youth Ministry ___

5. A sense of God's presence/atmosphere of your church ___

6. Pastor/Preaching —

7. Location of your church--major highway or thoroughfare; in the center of a new housing development, etc. —

8. Worship style/music —

9. A strong sense of "community" in your area--people support local businesses and attend local churches —

10. Sunday school organization —

11. The doctrinal position of your church —

12. Friendliness of members —

Please write the name of your church: _____

Please rate your church membership as predominately:
__ Blue-collar __ White-collar

Please write your name: _____

Please write your position/involvement in the church:

(Your personal comments are appreciated. Please use the back of this form to comment on your answers or to offer additional insights regarding the growth of your church.

Appendix B--TABLE OF RESPONSES

CALVARY BAPTIST CHURCH

Question	None	Minor	Moderate	Major	Total
1	1	1	0	0	2
2	0	1	1	0	2
3	0	2	0	0	2
4	0	1	0	1	2
5	0	0	0	2	2
6	0	0	0	2	2
7	0	2	0	0	2
8	0	1	1	0	2
9	0	2	0	0	2
10	1	1	0	0	2
11	0	2	0	0	2
12	0	0	2	0	2

DOUBLE SPRINGS BAPTIST

Question	None	Minor	Moderate	Major	Total
1	1	3	0	0	4
2	0	3	0	1	4
3	0	3	1	0	4
4	0	0	0	4	4
5	0	0	0	4	4
6	0	0	1	3	4
7	3	1	0	0	4
8	1	2	1	0	4
9	0	1	2	1	4
10	0	0	4	0	4
11	0	1	2	1	4
12	0	0	2	2	4

EAST CENTRE BAPTIST CHURCH

Question	None	Minor	Moderate	Major	Total
1	1	0	0	0	1
2	0	0	0	1	1
3	0	0	1	0	1
4	0	0	1	0	1
5	0	0	0	1	1
6	0	0	0	1	1
7	1	0	0	0	1
8	0	0	1	0	1
9	0	0	1	0	1
10	0	1	0	0	1
11	0	0	1	0	1
12	0	0	0	1	1

HILLSBORO BAPTIST CHURCH

Question	None	Minor	Moderate	Major	Total
1	3	0	0	0	3
2	0	2	1	0	3
3	0	0	2	1	3
4	0	0	2	1	3
5	0	0	0	3	3
6	0	0	0	3	3
7	2	1	0	0	3
8	0	0	2	1	3
9	1	2	0	0	3
10	0	1	2	0	3
11	0	0	2	1	3
12	0	0	0	3	3

JONESBORO BAPTIST

Question	None	Minor	Moderate	Major	Total
1	1	0	2	0	3
2	0	1	2	0	3
3	0	1	1	1	3
4	0	1	0	2	3
5	0	0	1	2	3
6	0	0	2	1	3
7	2	0	1	0	3
8	0	1	2	0	3
9	0	0	2	1	3
10	0	0	3	0	3
11	0	0	0	3	3
12	0	0	1	2	3

NEW PROSPECT BAPTIST

Question	None	Minor	Moderate	Major	Total
1	1	1	1	0	3
2	0	0	2	1	3
3	0	1	1	0	2
4	0	0	3	0	3
5	0	0	1	2	3
6	0	0	2	1	3
7	0	3	0	0	3
8	0	2	1	0	3
9	0	2	0	1	3
10	0	1	1	1	3
11	0	0	1	2	3
12	0	0	0	3	3

NEW ZION BAPTIST

Question	None	Minor	Moderate	Major	Total
1	1	1	0	1	3
2	0	1	2	0	3
3	0	0	1	2	3
4	0	0	2	1	3
5	0	0	0	3	3
6	0	0	1	2	3
7	2	0	1	0	3
8	0	0	1	2	3
9	0	0	1	2	3
10	0	1	2	0	3
11	0	1	0	2	3
12	0	0	0	3	3

NORTH RUSSELLVILLE BAPTIST

Question	None	Minor	Moderate	Major	Total
1	2	2	0	0	4
2	0	3	0	1	4
3	0	0	3	1	4
4	0	1	2	1	4
5	0	0	1	3	4
6	0	0	3	1	4
7	1	3	0	0	4
8	1	1	1	1	4
9	2	0	1	1	4
10	0	2	2	0	4
11	0	1	0	3	4
12	0	0	0	4	4

Appendix C--SAMPLE COMPUTATIONS

Symbols
x = mean
$\sum$ = sum of all responses
n = number of possible responses
s or σ = standard deviation

Calculation of Question Number One

$\bar{x} = \sum x/n = 11+8+3+1/4 = 5.75$

$s = \sqrt{\sum(x-\bar{x})^2/n-1}$

$s = \sqrt{[(11-5.75)^2+(8-5.75)+(3-5.75)^2+(1-5.75)^2/4-1]}$

$s = \sqrt{[(5.25)^2+(3.75)^2+(-2.75)^2+(-4.75)^2/3]}$

$s = \sqrt{[27.56 + 14.06 + 7.56 + 22.56}$

$s = \sqrt{[71.74/3]}$

$s = \sqrt{23.91}$

$s = 4.89$

$\sigma\bar{x} = s/\sqrt{n} = 4.89/\sqrt{4}$

$= 4.89/2 = 2.45$

Three (4-1) degrees of freedom at 90% confidence (see Appendix D) is 2.353

$2.353 \times \sigma\bar{x} = 2.353 \times 2.45 = 5.76$

Significant number $= \bar{x} + 5.76 = 5.75 + 5.76 = 11.51$

Appendix D--CRITICAL VALUES OF "t" [248]

Critical Values of t

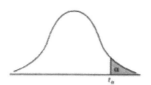

df	$t_{.100}$	$t_{.050}$	$t_{.025}$	$t_{.010}$	$t_{.005}$	$t_{.001}$	$t_{.0005}$
1	3.078	6.314	12.706	31.821	63.657	318.31	636.62
2	1.886	2.920	4.303	6.965	9.925	22.326	31.598
3	1.638	2.353	3.182	4.541	5.841	10.213	12.924
4	1.533	2.132	2.776	3.747	4.604	7.173	8.610
5	1.476	2.015	2.571	3.365	4.032	5.893	6.869
6	1.440	1.943	2.447	3.143	3.707	5.208	5.959
7	1.415	1.895	2.365	2.998	3.499	4.785	5.408
8	1.397	1.860	2.306	2.896	3.355	4.501	5.041
9	1.383	1.833	2.262	2.821	3.250	4.297	4.781
10	1.372	1.812	2.228	2.764	3.169	4.144	4.587
11	1.363	1.796	2.201	2.718	3.106	4.025	4.437
12	1.356	1.782	2.179	2.681	3.055	3.930	4.318
13	1.350	1.771	2.160	2.650	3.012	3.852	4.221
14	1.345	1.761	2.145	2.624	2.977	3.787	4.140
15	1.341	1.753	2.131	2.602	2.947	3.733	4.073
16	1.337	1.746	2.120	2.583	2.921	3.686	4.015
17	1.333	1.740	2.110	2.567	2.898	3.646	3.965
18	1.330	1.734	2.101	2.552	2.878	3.610	3.922
19	1.328	1.729	2.093	2.539	2.861	3.579	3.883
20	1.325	1.725	2.086	2.528	2.845	3.552	3.850
21	1.323	1.721	2.080	2.518	2.831	3.527	3.819
22	1.321	1.717	2.074	2.508	2.819	3.505	3.792
23	1.319	1.714	2.069	2.500	2.807	3.485	3.767
24	1.318	1.711	2.064	2.492	2.797	3.467	3.745
25	1.316	1.708	2.060	2.485	2.787	3.450	3.725
26	1.315	1.706	2.056	2.479	2.779	3.435	3.707
27	1.314	1.703	2.052	2.473	2.771	3.421	3.690
28	1.313	1.701	2.048	2.467	2.763	3.408	3.674
29	1.311	1.699	2.045	2.462	2.756	3.396	3.659
30	1.310	1.697	2.042	2.457	2.750	3.385	3.646
40	1.303	1.684	2.021	2.423	2.704	3.307	3.551
60	1.296	1.671	2.000	2.390	2.660	3.232	3.460
120	1.289	1.658	1.980	2.358	2.617	3.160	3.373
∞	1.282	1.645	1.960	2.326	2.576	3.090	3.291

[248]*Source:* Martin Sternstein, <u>Statistics</u> (Hauppauge, NY: Barron's Educational Services, 1994), 193.

Appendix E--
QUESTIONNAIRE FOR
TEAM MEMBERS

Church Name/Location: _____

Team Member Name(s): _____

Please take adequate notes so that you can explain your
viewpoint regarding this church. This form should be completed
and presented to the other team members at the group retreat.

The following four growth factors have been ranked by the
churches surveyed according to their impact on church growth.
Please circle the response that best describes your observation
using the following scale, and write your comments in the space
provided under each factor (give specific examples of the way
each factor contributed to the service):

1-insignificant   2-mildly significant
3-moderately significant   4-greatly significant

1. A sense of God's presence/atmosphere in the church 1 2 3 4

_____

2. Friendliness of members   1 2 3 4

_____

3. The doctrinal position of the church   1 2 3 4

_____

4. Pastor/Preaching   1 2 3 4

_____

Appendix F--AGENDA FOR TEAM MEMBERS

Twenty-three church leaders representing eight growing rural churches rated the significance of twelve factors in the growth of their churches. Tonight, we are looking at number one--the presence of God in the church found in Matthew 18:15-20.

Jesus promises His presence in verse 20. What are the three conditions for His coming into a worship service?

I. Corporate Purity (vv. 15-18)

    A. Go by yourself

    B. Take others with you

    C. Take them before the church leaders

    D. Treat them as an outsider

II. Corporate Prayer (vs. 19)

III. Corporate Participation (vs. 20)

Appendix G—SERMONS

SERMON ONE--GOD'S PRESENCE IN THE CHURCH

Our objectives are to:

1. Review the four growth principles

2. Learn how application other churches are currently applying these principles

3. Rating our church with regard to the four principles

4. Agree on ways to apply the principles to improve our church

Friday Evening

6:00-6:45	Supper (provided by the church)
6:45-7:00	Prayer
7:00-9:00	Defining the four Growth Principles

Saturday Morning

7:15-7:45	Breakfast (provided by the church)
7:45-8:00	Prayer
8:00-9:15	Large Group Sharing Time—What did we observe at the 7 churches?
9:15-10:30	Small Group Discussion—3 groups
	1. Discuss: How does our church rate with regard to the four areas
	2. What are some concrete steps we can take to improve in each of the four areas?
	3. How can this group/team assist in the implementation of these principles?
10:30-11:30	Large Group Recommendations--limited to 20 minutes per group
11:30-12:00	Individual assignments and prayer
12:00 noon	Dismiss

SERMON TWO: FRIENDLINESS OF THE CHURCH MEMBERS

Twenty-three church leaders representing eight growing rural churches rated the significance of twelve factors in the growth of their churches. Tonight, we are looking at number two--the principles that produce friendliness in the lives of church members found in   Romans 12:9-13:

I.   Sensitivity (vs. 9)--sincere love

II. Submission

     A. To other Christians (vs. 10)

     B. To Christ Himself (vv. 11-12)

III. Sacrifice (vs. 13a)

IV. Skill (vs. 13b)

SERMON THREE: THE DOCTRINAL POSITION OF THE CHURCH

Twenty-three church leaders representing eight growing rural churches rated the significance of twelve factors in the growth of their churches. Tonight, we are looking at number three--the importance of the Doctrinal Position (scriptural stand) of the Church. Effective doctrine, according to 2 Timothy 4:1-3, must be accompanied by:

I.   Thoughtfulness (vs. 1)--considering the Lord

II. Tirelessness (vs. 2)--regarding the Bible

III. Timeliness (vs. 3)--a limited time frame

SERMON FOUR: THE PASTOR AND PREACHING

Twenty-three church leaders representing eight growing rural churches rated the significance of twelve factors in the growth of their churches. Tonight, we are counting down from number four--the importance of the Pastor and Preaching found in Romans 10:14-15.

I. Nine needs of people:

Preaching that teaches the Bible; preaching that applies to my life; the pastor is a "real" person; the pastor is a person of conviction; personal contact by the pastor; the pastor is a good communicator in and out of the pulpit; the pastor is a good leader; and a Pastor's Class (Sunday school, etc.).[20]

II. Four needs of a pastor:

A. A Congregation (vs. 14a)--an audience

B. A Communication (vs. 14b)--a message

C. A Consecration (vs. 15a)--authorization to represent the Lord

D. A Commendation (vs. 15b)--the welcome of those who receive the Word

SELECTED BIBLIOGRAPHY

Books

1971 Directory of the First Baptist Church of Town Creek, Alabama. Waco, TX: United Church Directories, 1971.

Adams, Jay E. <u>Competent to Counsel</u>. Grand Rapids: Zondervan, 1970.

Anderson, Leith. Dying for Change: An Arresting Look at the New Realities Confronting Churches and Para-Church Ministries. Minneapolis: Bethany House, 1990.

Anderson, Leith, Jack Hayford, and Ben Patterson. Who's In Charge? Standing Up to Leadership Pressures. Sisters, OR: Multnomah, 1993.

Arn, Win. "Evangelism or Disciple Making?" Church Growth: State of the Art. C. Peter Wagner, ed. Wheaton, IL: Tyndale, 1986.

Barna, George. Building Effective Lay Leadership Teams. Ventura, CA: Issachar Resources, 2001.

_____. Evangelism That Works: How to Reach Changing Generations with the Unchanging Gospel. Ventura, CA: Regal, 1995.

_____. Re-Churching the Unchurched. Ventura, CA: Issachar Resources, 2000.

_____. User Friendly Churches: What Christians Need To Know About the Churches People Love To Go To. Ventura, CA: Regal, 1991.

Benner, David G., ed. Baker Encyclopedia of
Psychology. Grand Rapids: Baker,
1985.

Biehl, Bobb. Stop Setting Goals If You Would
Rather Solve Problems. Nashville:
Moorings, Random House, 1995.

Biskupic, Joan. "School Prayer Rejected: High
Court Bans Student-led Acts." USA
Today. 20 June 2000. Sec. A. Ventura,
CA: Regal, 1991.

Boehm, Pegge, Deborah Cronin, Gary Farley, C.
Dean Freudenberger, Judith Bortner
Heffernam, Shannon Jung, Sandra
LeBlanc, Edward L. Queen, II, and David
C. Ruesink. Rural Ministry: The Shape of
the Renewal to Come. Nashville:
Abingdon, 1998.

Bolton, Robert. People Skills. New York: Simon
and Schuster, 1979.

Book of Memories. Town Creek, AL: The
Welcome Home Committee, 1989.

Bowman, Ray and Eddy Hall. When Not to Build: An Architect's Unconventional Wisdom for the Growing Church. Grand Rapids: Baker, 1992.

Callahan, Kennon L. Twelve Keys to an Effective Church: Strategic Planning for Mission. San Francisco, CA: Harper Collins, 1983.

Carter, Les and Jim Underwood. The Significance Principle: The Secret Behind High Performance People and Organizations. Nashville: Broadman and Holman, 1998.

Crabb, Larry. Understanding People. Grand Rapids: Zondevan, 1987.

Cymbala, Jim. Fresh Wind, Fresh Fire: What Happens When God's Spirit Invades the Hearts of His People. Grand Rapids: Zondervan, 1997.

Davis, Ron Lee. Mistreated. Portland, OR: Multnomah, 1989.

Dewey, John C. Human Nature and Conduct.
New York: Modern

Library, 1930). In Robert Bolton, People Skills.
New York: Simon and Schuster, Inc., 1979;
reprint, New York: Touchstone, 1986.

Fee, Gordon D. and Douglas Stewart. How to
Read the Bible for All Its Worth. Grand
Rapids: Zondervan, 1993.

Fields, Doug. Purpose Driven Youth Ministry:
Nine Essential Foundations for Healthy
Growth. Grand Rapids: Zondervan, 1998.

Fogiel, M. Super Review of Statistics.
Piscataway, NJ: Research and Education
Association, 2002.

Fowler, Harry H. Breaking Barriers of New
Church Growth: Increasing Attendance
from 0-150. Rocky Mount, NC: Creative
Growth Dynamics, 1988.

Freeman, John D. Country Church: Its Problems
and Their Solution. Atlanta: Home
Mission Board, 1943.

Gore, William J. and Leroy C. Hodapp, eds. Change in the Small Community: An Interdisciplinary Survey. New York: Friendship, 1967.

Hemphill, Ken and Bill Taylor. Ten Best Practices To Make Your Sunday School Work. Nashville: Lifeway, 2001.

Hemfelt, Robert, Frank Minirth, and Paul Meier. Love is a   Choice. Nashville: Thomas Nelson, 1989.

Johnson, Laney L. The Church: God's People on Mission.   Nashville: Convention, 1995.

Jones, Ezra Earl. Strategies for New Churches. New York: Harper and Row, 1976.

Kaiser, Walter C. Toward an Exegetical Theology. Grand   Rapids: Baker, 1981.

Maxwell, John C. Developing the Leaders Around You: How to Help Others Reach Their Full Potential. Nashville: Thomas Nelson, 1995.

_____. Developing the Leader Within You. Nashville: Thomas Nelson, 1993.

_____. Partners In Prayer: Support and Strengthen Your Pastor and Church Leaders. Nashville: Thomas Nelson, 1996.

_____. The 21 Irrefutable Laws of Leadership: Follow Them and People Will Follow You. Nashville: Thomas Nelson, 1998.

_____. Ushers and Greeters. El Cajon, CA: INJOY   Ministries, 1991.

McDonald, Gordon. Rebuilding Your Broken World. Nashville: Oliver-Nelson, 1988.

McGavran, Donald A. and Winfield C. Arn. Ten Steps for Church Growth. San Francisco, CA: Eerdmans, 1990.

McGavran, Donald A. Understanding Church Growth. 3d ed. Rev. and ed. C. Peter Wagner. Grand Rapids: Eerdmans, 1990.

McGee, Robert S. The Search for Significance. Nashville: Lifeway, 1992.

McIntosh, Gary L. The Exodus Principle: A Five-Part   Strategy to Free Your People for Ministry. Nashville: Broadman and Holman, 1995.

Merriam Webster's Collegiate Dictionary, 10th ed. Springfield, MA: Merriam-Webster, 1995.

Miller, James B. The Corporate Coach. New York: St. Martin's, 1993.

Owens, Buddy. The Way of a Worshiper: Discover the Secret of Friendship with God. San Clemente, CA: Maranatha, 2002.

Pearson, E. S. "Student": A Statistical Biography of William Sealy Gosset. eds. R. L. Plackett and G. A. Barnard. Oxford, England: Clarendon, 1990.

Professional Sales Development--Phase I: You and Your Family. U.S.A.: Metropolitan Life Insurance Company,   1976.

Rainer, Thom S. Eating the Elephant: Bite-Sized Steps To Achieve Long-Term Growth In Your Church. Nashville: Broadman and Holman, 1994.

_____. Effective Evangelistic Churches. Nashville: Broadman and Holman, 1996.

_____. Surprising Insights From the Unchurched and Proven Ways To Reach Them. Grand Rapids: Zondervan, 2001.

Sande, Ken. The Peacemaker. Grand Rapids: Baker, 1991.

Schaller, Lyle E. Growing Plans. Nashville: Abingdon, 1981.

Seamands, David A. Living With Your Dreams. Wheaton, IL: Victor, 1990.

Smith, Rockwell C. Rural Ministry and the Changing Community. Nashville: Abindgon, 1971.

Sternstein, Martin. Statistics. Hauppauge, NY: Barron's, 1994.

Strobel, Lee. Inside the Mind of Unchurched Harry and Mary: How To Reach Friends and Family Who Avoid God and the Church. Grand Rapids: Zondervan, 1993.

Sweet, Leonard. Soul Tsunami: Sink or Swim in New Millenium Culture. Grand Rapids: Zondervan, 1999.

Thomas, Robert L. "Exegesis and Expository Preaching." In   Rediscovering Expository Preaching. Ed. Richard L. Mayhue. Dallas, TX: Word, 1992.

Torrey, R. A. The Power of Prayer. Grand Rapids: Zondervan, 1971.

Wagner, C. Peter. Leading Your Church to Growth: The Secret of Pastor/People Partnership in Dynamic Church Growth. Ventura, CA: Regal, 1984.

_____. The Church Growth Survey Handbook. 3d ed. Colorado Springs, CO: Global Church Growth, 1984.

_____. Your Church Can Grow: Seven Vital Signs of a Healthy Church, second edition. Ventura, CA: Regal, 1984.

Warren, Rick. The Purpose Driven Church: Growth Without Compromising Your Message and Mission. Grand Rapids: Zondervan, 1995.

Welch, Bobby H. Evangelism Through the Sunday School: A Journey of FAITH. Nashville: Lifeway, 1999.

Welch, Jack with John A. Byrne. Jack: Straight from the Gut. New York: Warner, 2001.

White, James Emery. Opening the Front Door: Worship and Church Growth. Nashville: Convention, 1992.

Ziglar, Zig. See You at the Top. Gretna, LA: Pelican, 1975.

Interviews

Cross, Jackie. Interview by author, 24 October
        2000, Town   Creek, AL. Handwritten

Smith, Tommy. Interview by author, 25 October
        2000, Town   Creek, AL. Handwritten
        notes.

Yates, John. Interview by author, 10 November
        2000, Town   Creek, AL. Handwritten
        notes.

Newspapers

"Effective Churches: Barna Reveals Church
        Habits Necessary for Greater
        Effectiveness in Ministry." The Alabama
        Baptist. 7 May 1998.

Jenkins, Edwin F. "The Altitude of Church Growth: An Issue of Attitude or Aptitude?" The Alabama Baptist. 30 April 1998.

Johnson, Doug. "Sun Belt Prosperous, Poor." The Decatur Daily. 1 September 2002.

Stovall, Terry. "A Study of the Differences Between Growing, Declining, Plateaued and Erratic Growth of Southern Baptist Churches in Texas," The Alabama Baptist, 7 February 2002.

Terry, Bob. "Ten Tips Identified For Postmodern Worship." The Alabama Baptist 12 April 2001.

Periodicals

Arn, Charles. "Second Impressions: Your Church Passed Their First Visit, But Will They Come Back?" Leadership Journal. Summer 2002.

Barna, George. "Barna's Most Intriguing Findings." On Mission. May-June 2002.

Burge, Gary M. "Are Evangelicals Missing God at Church?" Christianity Today. 6 October 1997.

Dotson, James. "Crossover Presents Varied Opportunities for Volunteers to Share Faith in Orlando." Baptist Press. Nashville: Baptist Press. 22 February 2000.

Ellsworth, Tim. "Baptists Adrift In Doctrinal Confusion. SBC LIFE. October 2001.

"Honor Your Pastor!" SBC LIFE. October 2001.

"How The Family Church Grows: Honest Talk About Leading Change In The Smaller Congregation." Leadership Journal. XIX. Spring 1998.

Karon, Jan. "Praying In Prime Time." World Vision Today. Autumn 2002.

Leiblich, Julia. "Southern Baptist President Urges Outreach." Athens Daily News. 16 June 1999.

McIntosh, Gary L. "Biblical Church Growth: Growing Faithful Churches In the Third Millenium." Journal Of Evangelism And Missions. 1. Spring 2002.

Reiland, Dan. "Mergers and Turnarounds (Part Two)." The Pastor's Coach: Equipping the Leaders of Today's Church. Vol. III, No. 18.

Schaller, Lyle E. "Will the Circle Be Broken?" Leadership Journal. Summer 1998. Vol. XIX, No. 3.

_____. "You Can't Believe Everything You Hear About Church Growth: Busting Common Myths About Expansion and Change." Christianity Today. Winter 1997.

Wagner, C. Peter and Richard L. Gorsuch. "The Quality Church (Part 1)." Leadership. Winter 1983.

Yarborough, Charles. "Hope In A No-growth Town: Realistic Help for Churches Facing Seemingly Impossible Odds." Leadership Journal. Summer 1996.

Published Reports

2001 Annual Of the Alabama Baptist State Convention. Montgomery, AL: Alabama Baptist State Board of Missions, 2002.

ACLU Position Paper. New York, NY: American Civil Liberties Union. Fall 1999.

"Americans United Advises Pennsylvania Board of Education   to Reject Creationist Science Standards." AUCS News Brief. 4 December 2000.

AWANA Clubs International. AWANA: Who We Are, What We Do. Streamwood, IL: AWANA Website Online. 2002.

Barna, George. "Americans Draw Theological Beliefs from Diverse Points of View." The Barna Update, a bi-weekly email from George Barna. Ventura, CA: Barna Research, 8 October 2002.

Barna, George R. "The Faith of Hispanics is Shifting." The Barna Update, a bi-weekly email from George Barna.   Ventura, CA: Barna Research. 3 January 2001.

Department of Geography, College of Arts and Sciences. Population Density Map. Tuscaloosa, AL: University of Alabama, 2000.

"Federal Court of Appeals Strikes Down Government Display of Ten Commandments." AUCS News Brief. 13 December   2000.

Jones, Philip B. Southern Baptist Congregations Today. Atlanta, GA: North American Mission Board. 2001.

LifeWay Christian Resources. Annual Church Profile. Nashville: Southern Baptist Directory Services Online, 2001.

Membership Statement. Washington, DC: Americans United for   Separation of Church and State.

"Religious Liberty." Our Issues. Washington, DC: People for the American Way, 2000-1981.

Report of the Baptist Faith and Message Study Committee to the Southern Baptist Convention. Orlando, FL: Southern Baptist Convention. 14 June 2000.

U.S. Department of Commerce. 1989 Income and Poverty Status, Town Creek, AL. Washington, DC: American FactFinder Website Online, 1996.

U.S. Department of Commerce. 1990 Labor Force Status and Employment Characteristics, Town Creek, AL.   Washington, DC: American FactFinder Website Online, 1996.

U.S. Department of Commerce. 1990 Social
     Characteristics, Town Creek, AL.
     Washington, DC: American FactFinder
     Website Online, 1996.

U.S. Department of Commerce. 2000 Census of
     Population. Washington, D.C.: U.S.
     Census Bureau Online, 2000.

U.S. Department of Commerce. General
     Population and Housing Characteristics,
     Town Creek, AL. Washington, DC:
     American FactFinder Website Online,
     1996.

U. S. Department of Commerce. Population
     Estimates for the Years 1994-1999 for
     Town Creek, AL. Washington, DC: U.S.
     Census Bureau Online. 20 October 2000.

U. S. Department of Commerce. U.S. Gazetteer.
     Washington, DC: U.S. Census Bureau
     Online. 20 October 2000.

U. S. Department of Commerce. Urban and
     Rural Definitions. Washington, DC: U.S.
     Census Bureau Online, 1995.

Winter, William F. The State of the South 2002:
        Shadows in the Sunbelt Revisited.
        Chapel-Hill, NC: MDC Inc., 2002.

Specialized Dictionaries

Grimm, [Carl Ludwig] and [Christian Gottlob]
        Wilke. Greek-English Lexicon of the New
        Testament. trans. and rev. Joseph Henry
        Thayer. New York: American Book Co.,
        1889. reprint. Grand Rapids: Zondervan,
        1981.

Harris, R. Laird and Gleason L. Archer, Jr., and
        Bruce K. Waltke, eds. Theological
        Wordbook of the Old Testament. vol. A.
        Chicago: Moody, 1980.

Unpublished Surveys

Moore, W. Scott. "Growth Survey." Town Creek, AL: First Baptist Church, 2002.

South, Gail. Open Forum Meeting, 7 October 2002, Town Creek, AL. Handwritten notes.

3232325R00124

Printed in Great Britain
by Amazon.co.uk, Ltd.,
Marston Gate.